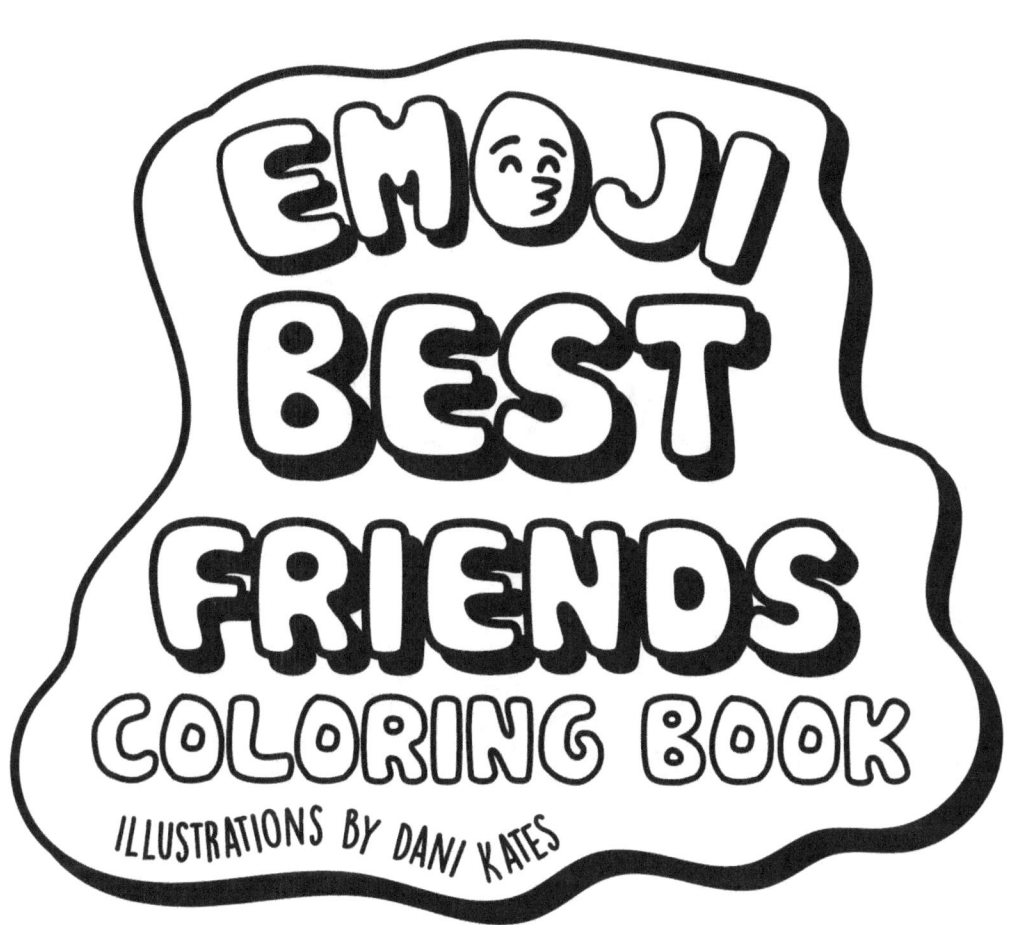

EMOJI BEST FRIENDS COLORING BOOK

ILLUSTRATIONS BY DANI KATES

36 PAGE COLORING BOOK

18 DESIGNS x 2 COPIES OF EACH

COLOR with

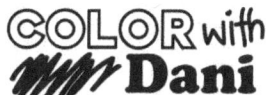

Dani

BEST FRIENDS

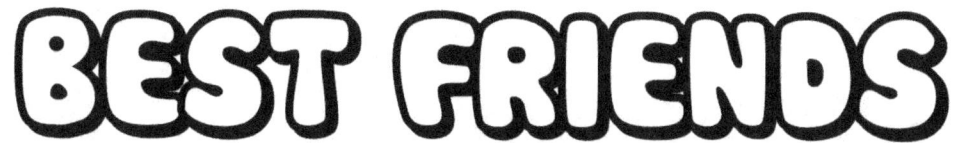

OMG, YOU ARE GOING TO LOOOOVE THIS COLORING BOOK...
IT'S ALL ABOUT EMOJIS AND BEST FRIENDS.

THIS COLORING BOOK IS DESIGNED FOR BEST FRIENDS.

THERE ARE TWO COPIES OF EACH PAGE.
(SO YOU CAN KEEP ONE FOR YOURSELF AND GIVE ONE TO YOUR BFF)

SOME PAGES HAVE A LINE RIGHT DOWN THE MIDDLE
SO YOU CAN CUT IT IN HALF AND GIVE HALF TO YOUR BFF.

YOU CAN SHARE AND COLOR THIS BOOK WITH MORE THAN JUST ONE BFF.
THERE ARE ENOUGH PAGES TO SHARE WITH 18 OF YOUR BEST FRIENDS.

3 FUN WAYS TO USE THIS BOOK:

① COLOR 2 COPIES OF ONE PICTURE
(KEEP ONE FOR YOURSELF AND GIVE ONE TO YOUR BFF AS A GIFT)

② YOU AND YOUR BFF EACH COLOR A COPY OF THE SAME PAGE.
SEE HOW SIMILAR OR DIFFERENT YOU CHOSE TO COLOR THEM.
(OR HAVE A COLORING CONTEST)

③ SOMETIMES WE MAKE MISTAKES WHEN WE'RE COLORING
AND WISH THAT WE COULD RE-DO IT.
NOW YOU CAN SINCE THERE ARE TWO COPIES OF EVERY PICTURE.

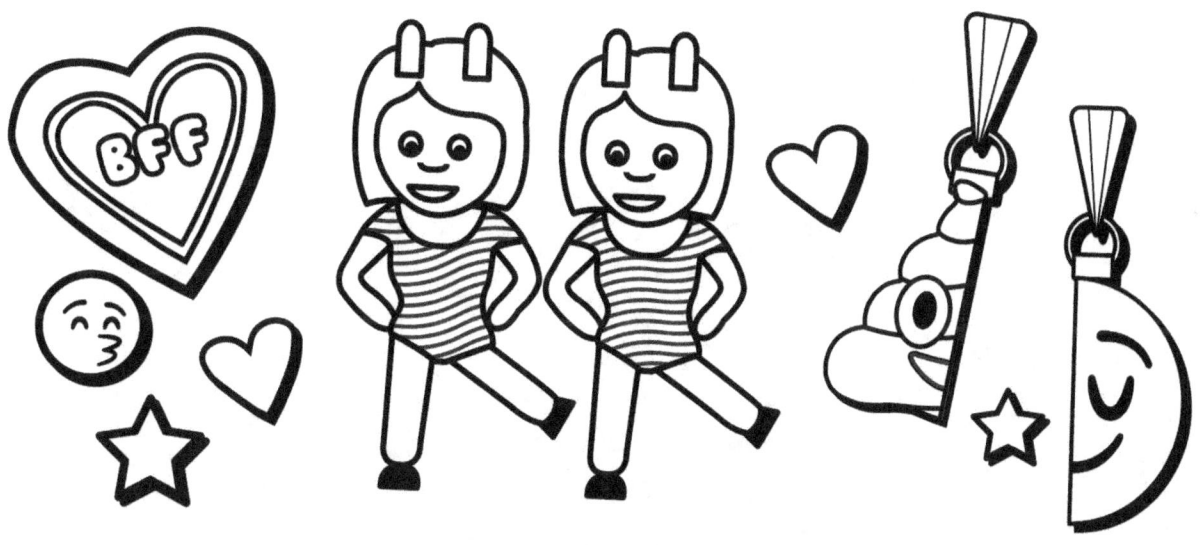

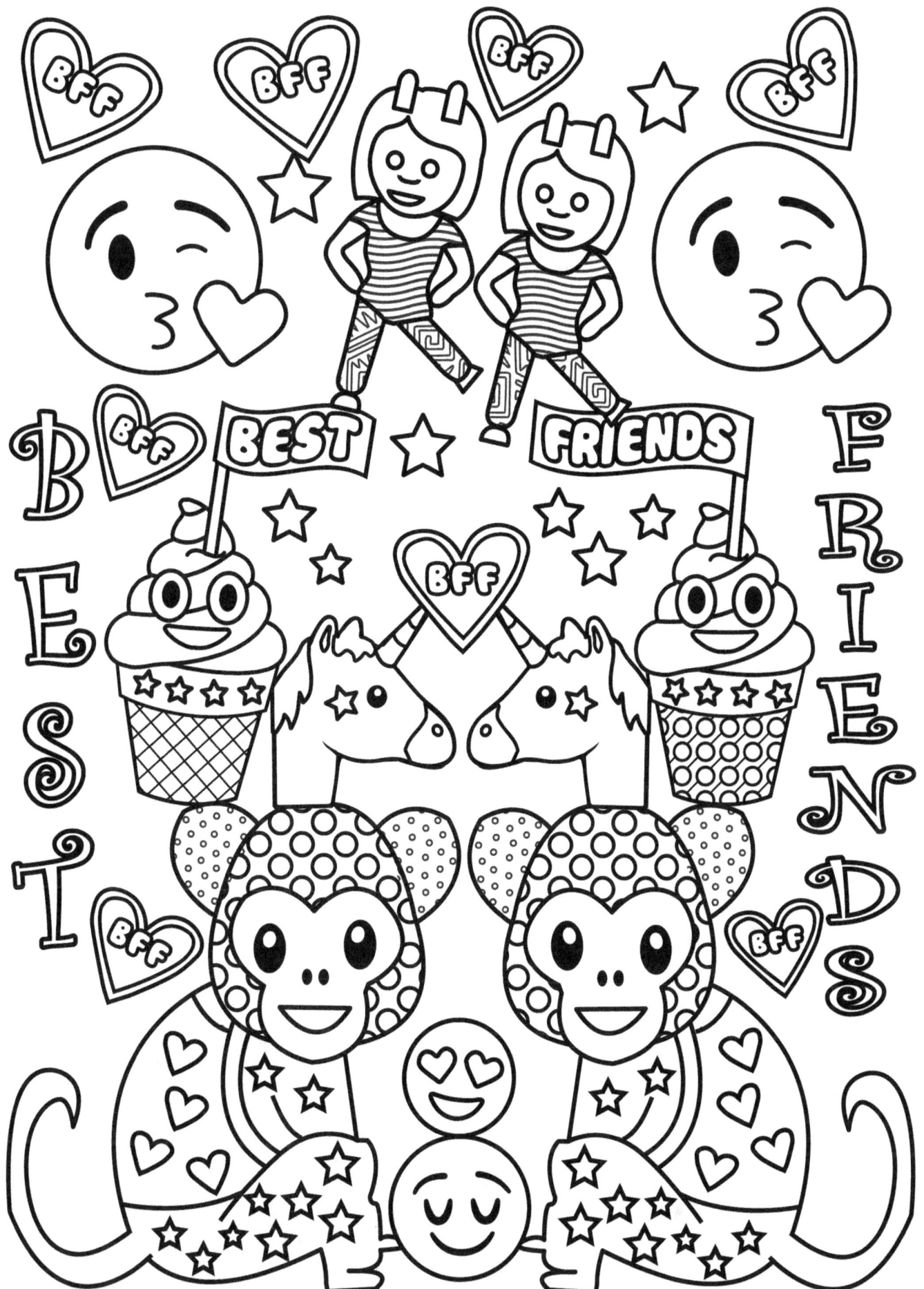

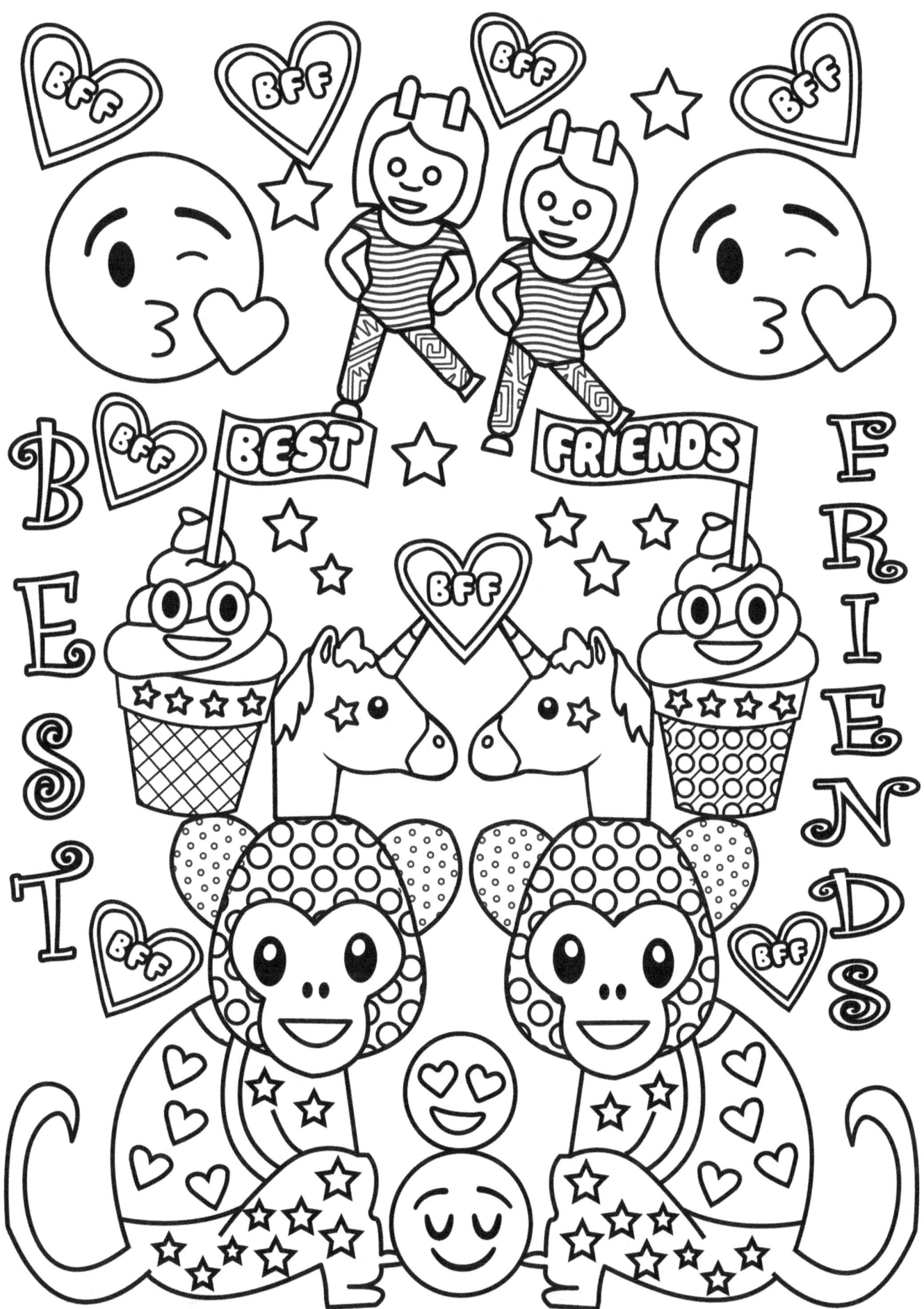

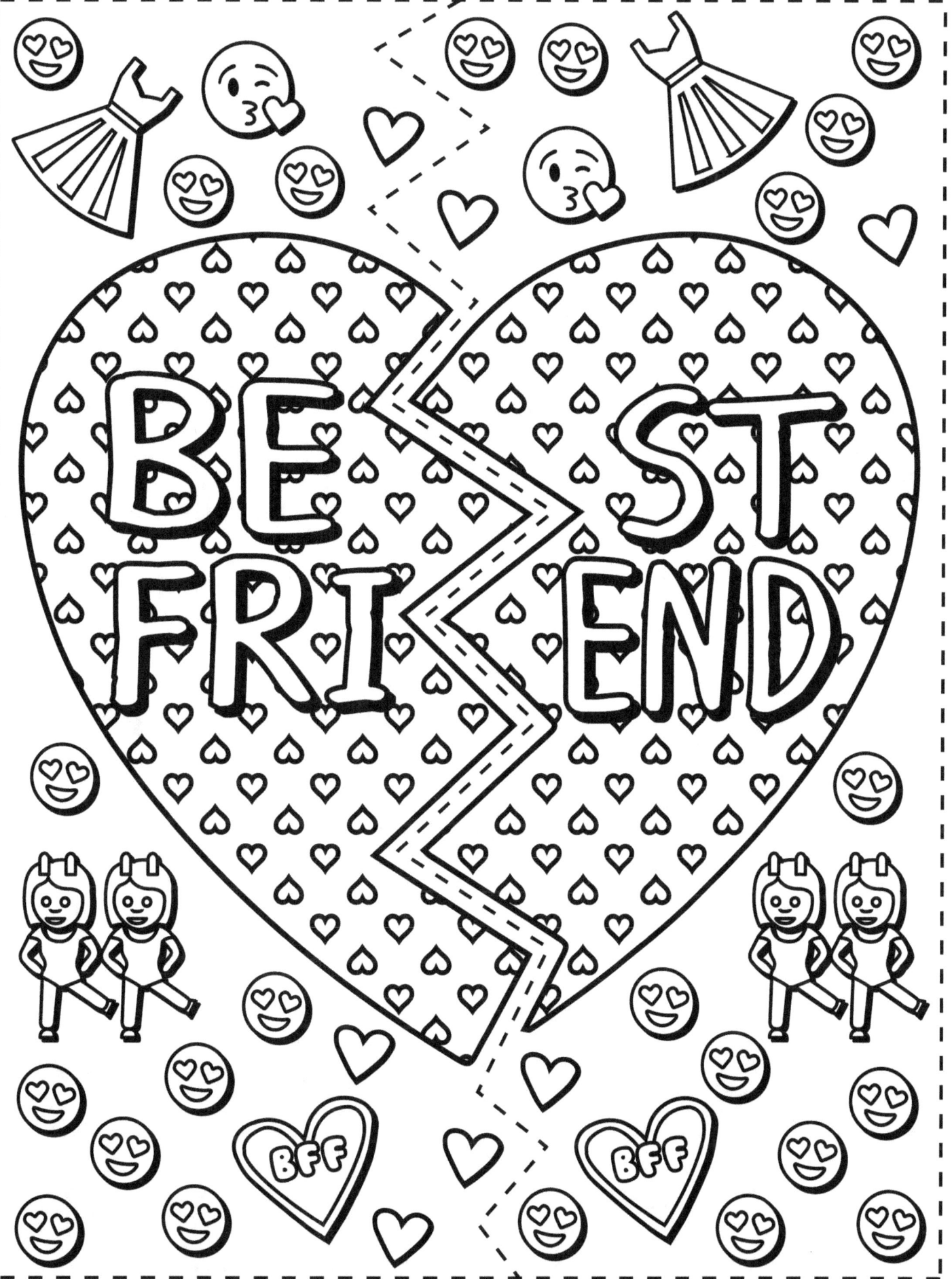

Cut along the dotted line (half for you half for a friend!)

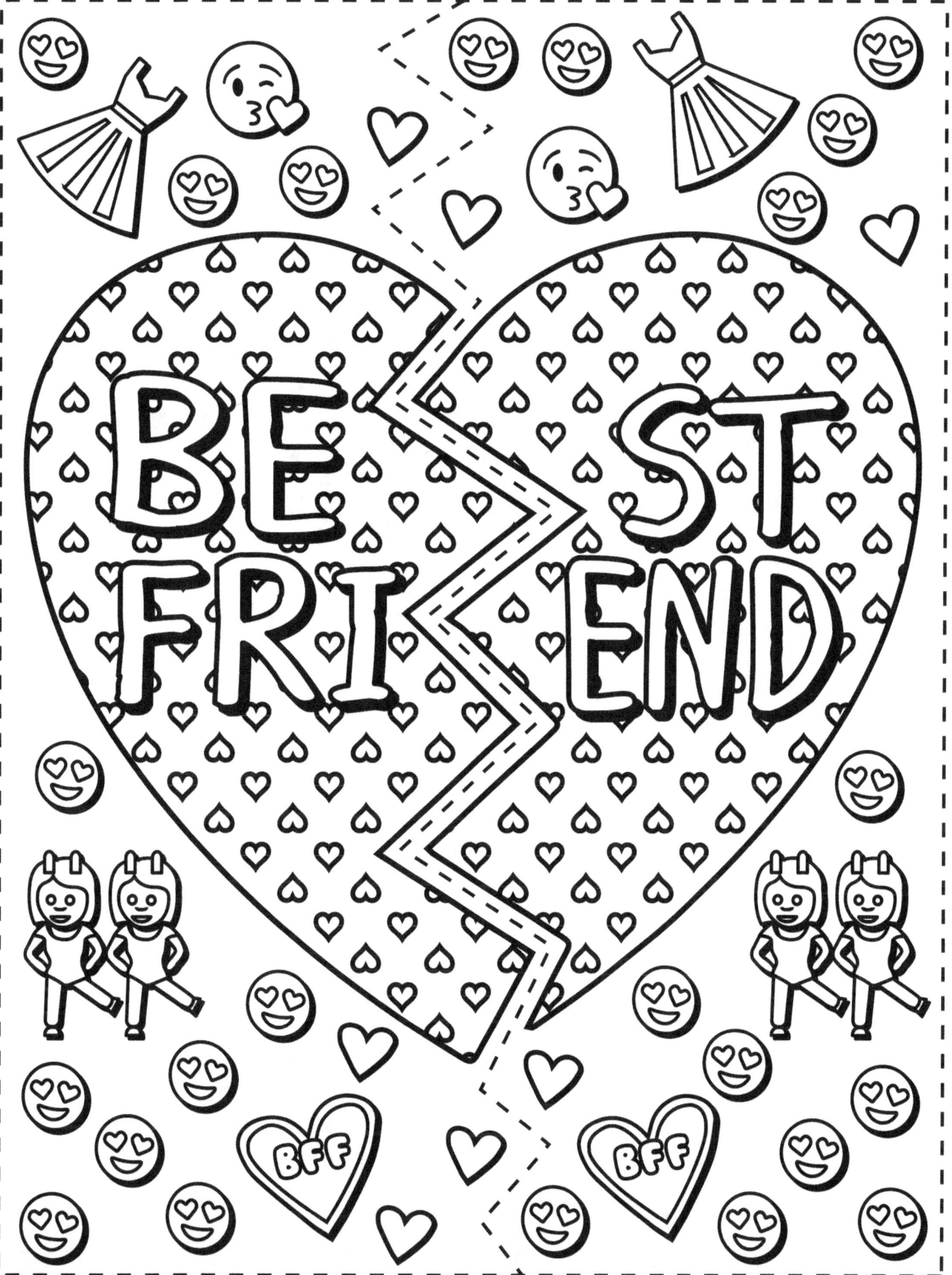

Cut along the dotted line (half for you half for a friend!)

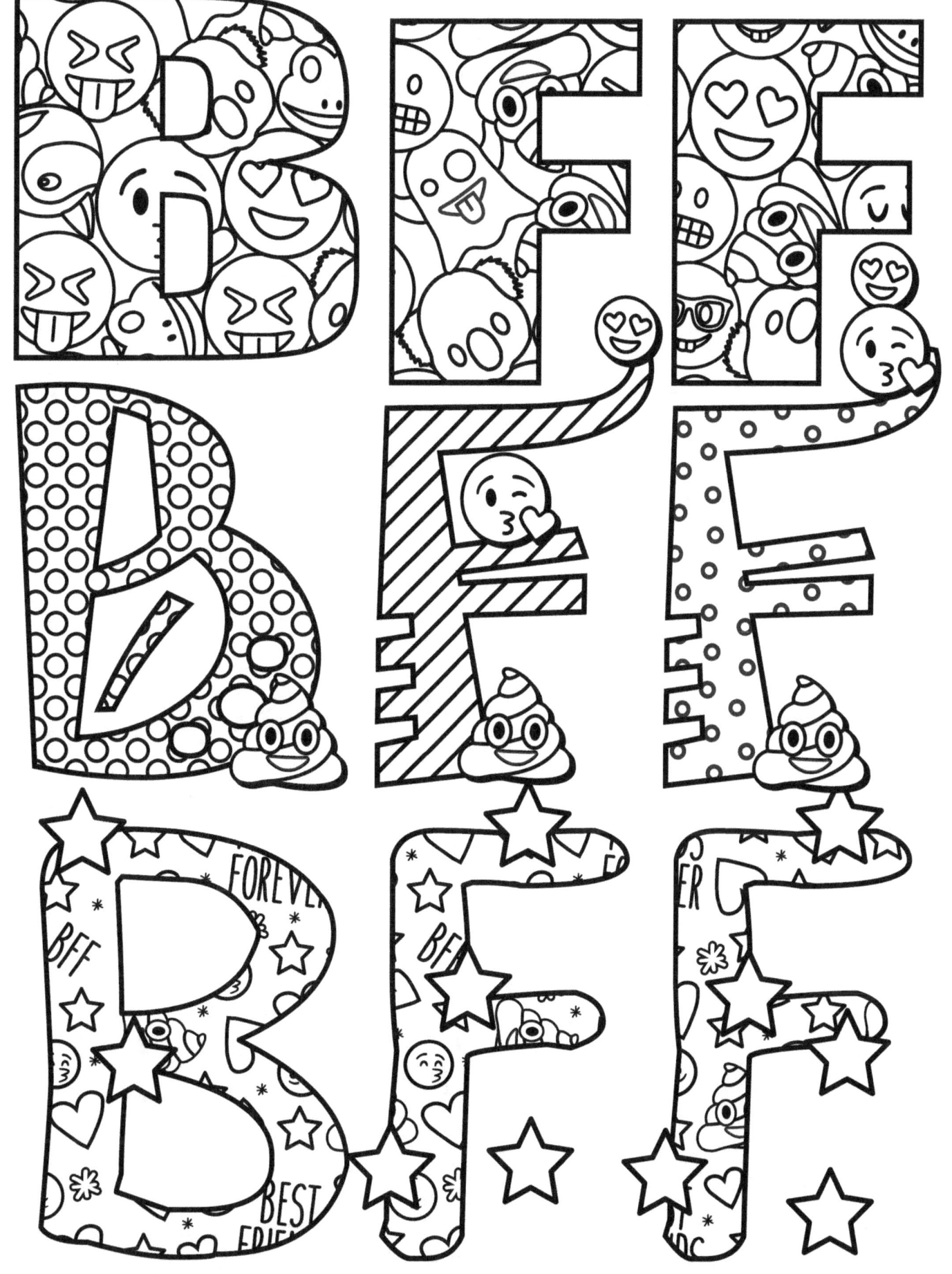

cut along the dotted line. one for you one for me

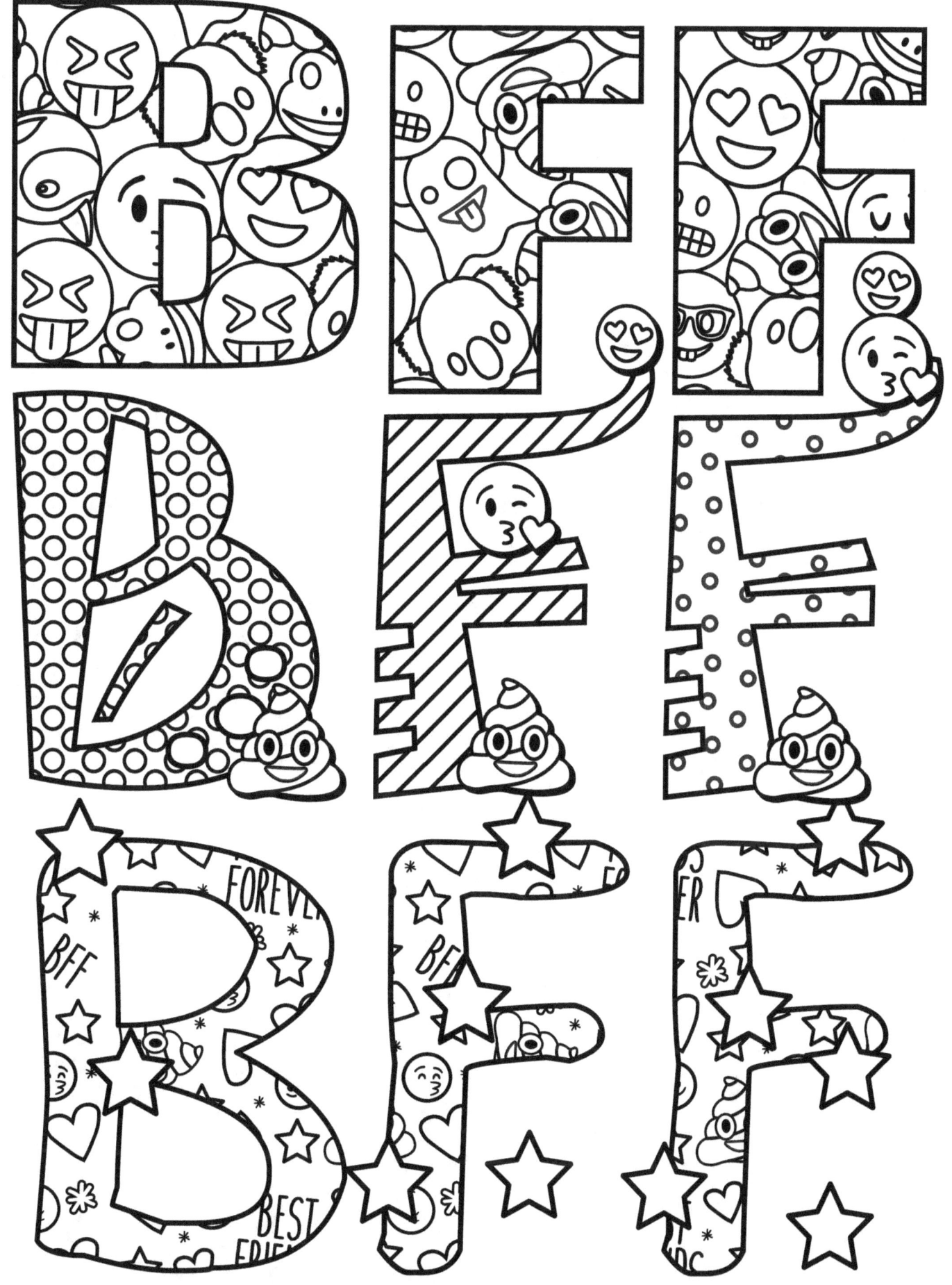

cut along the dotted line. one for you one for me

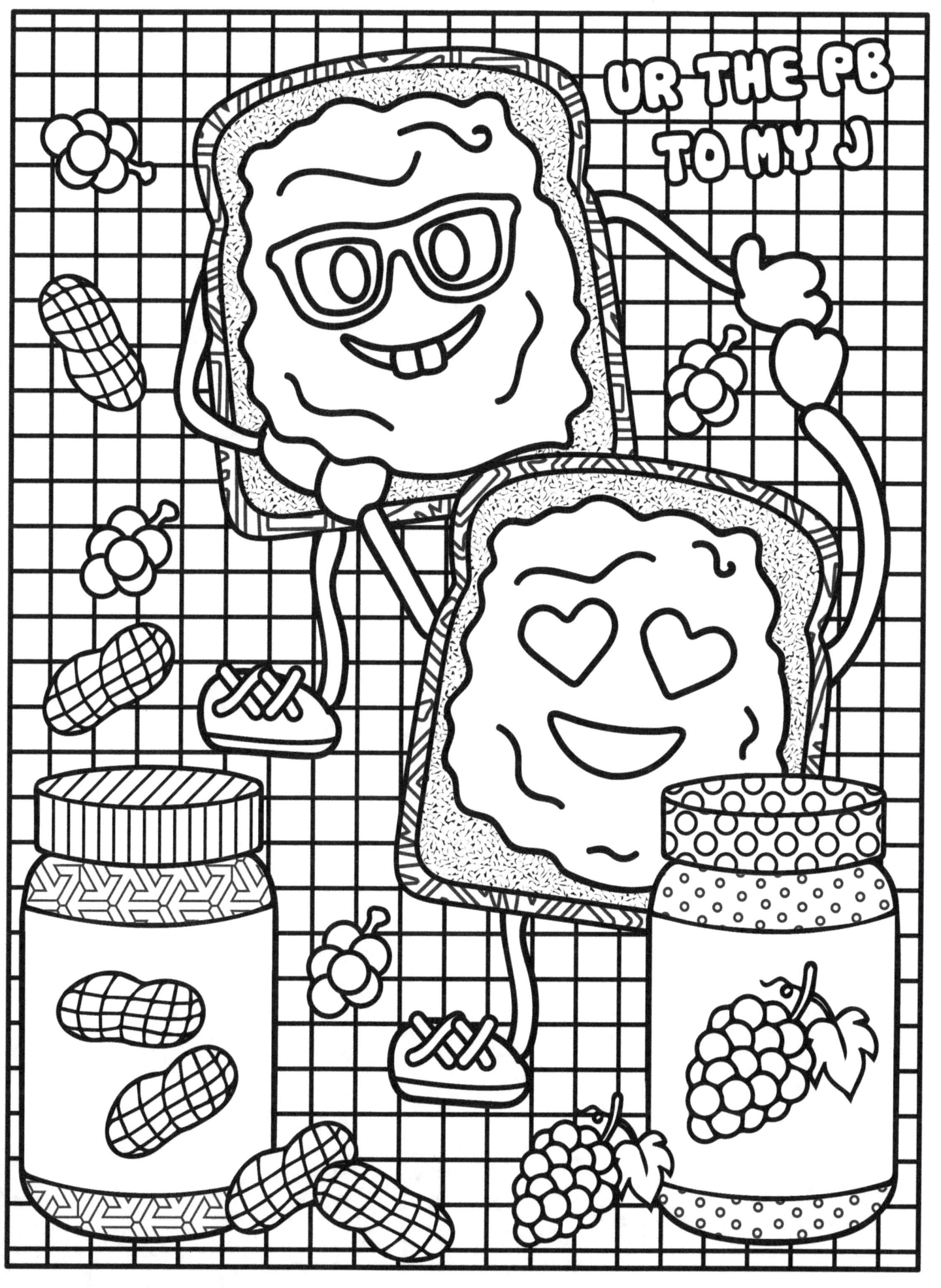

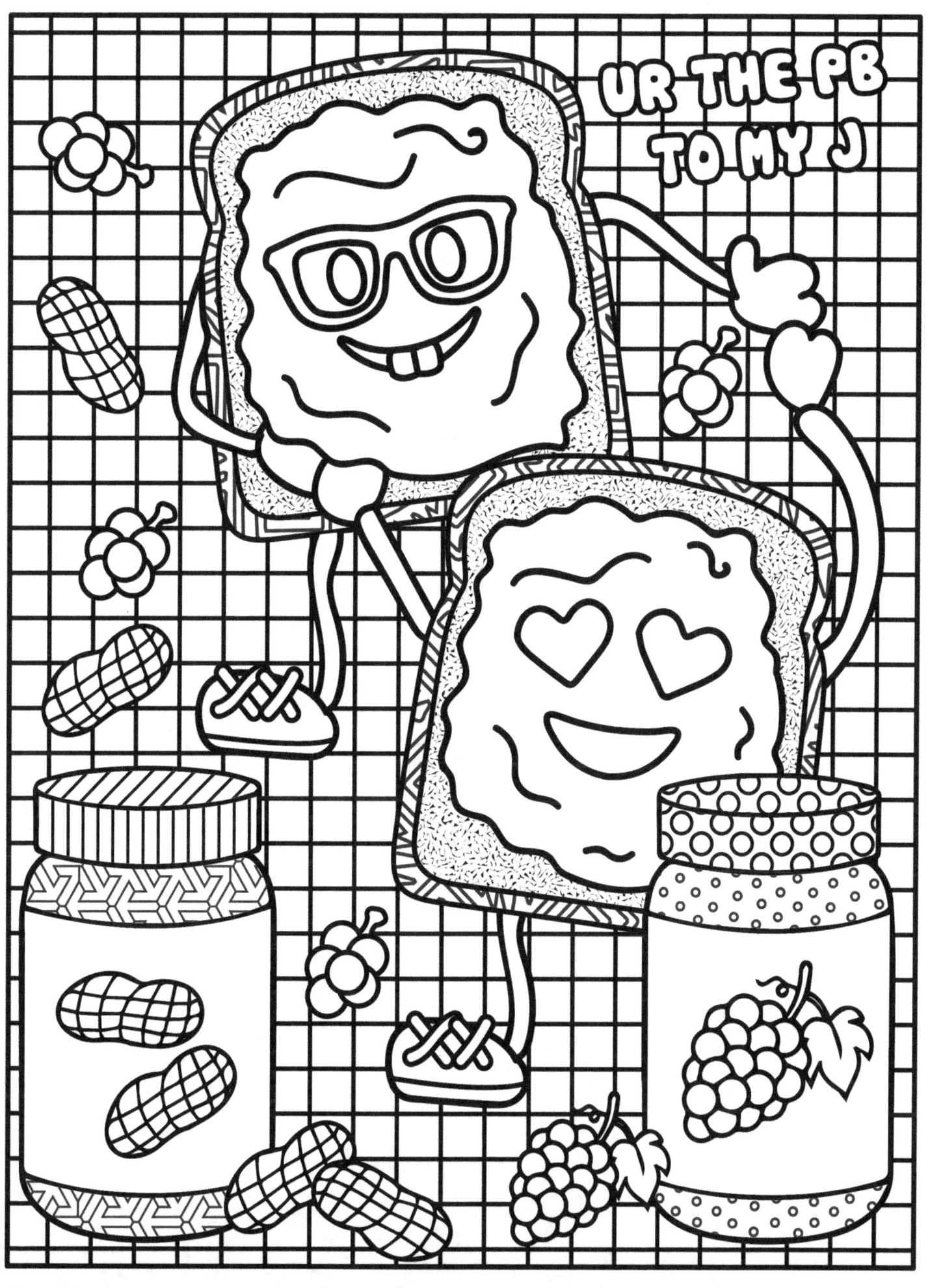

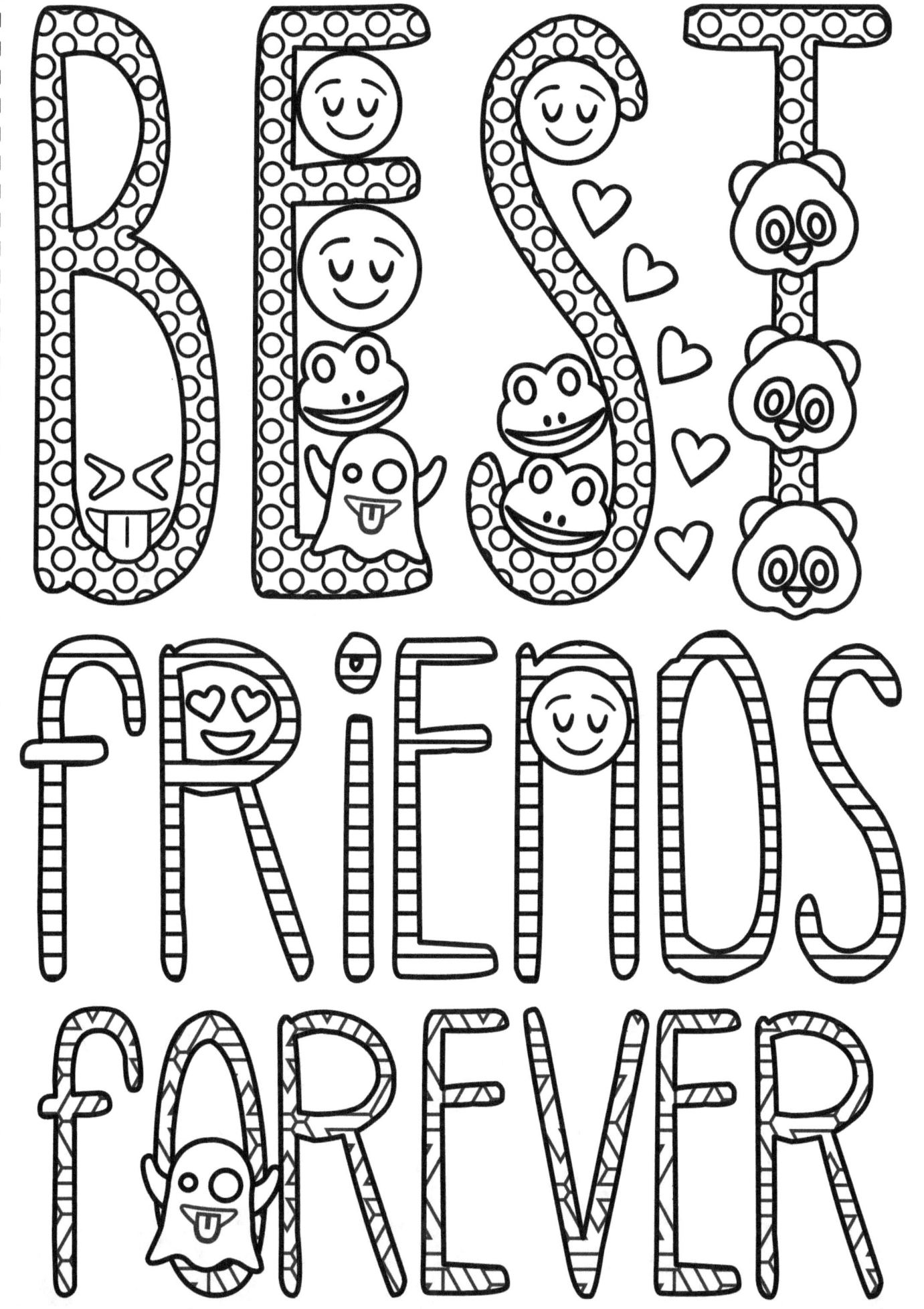

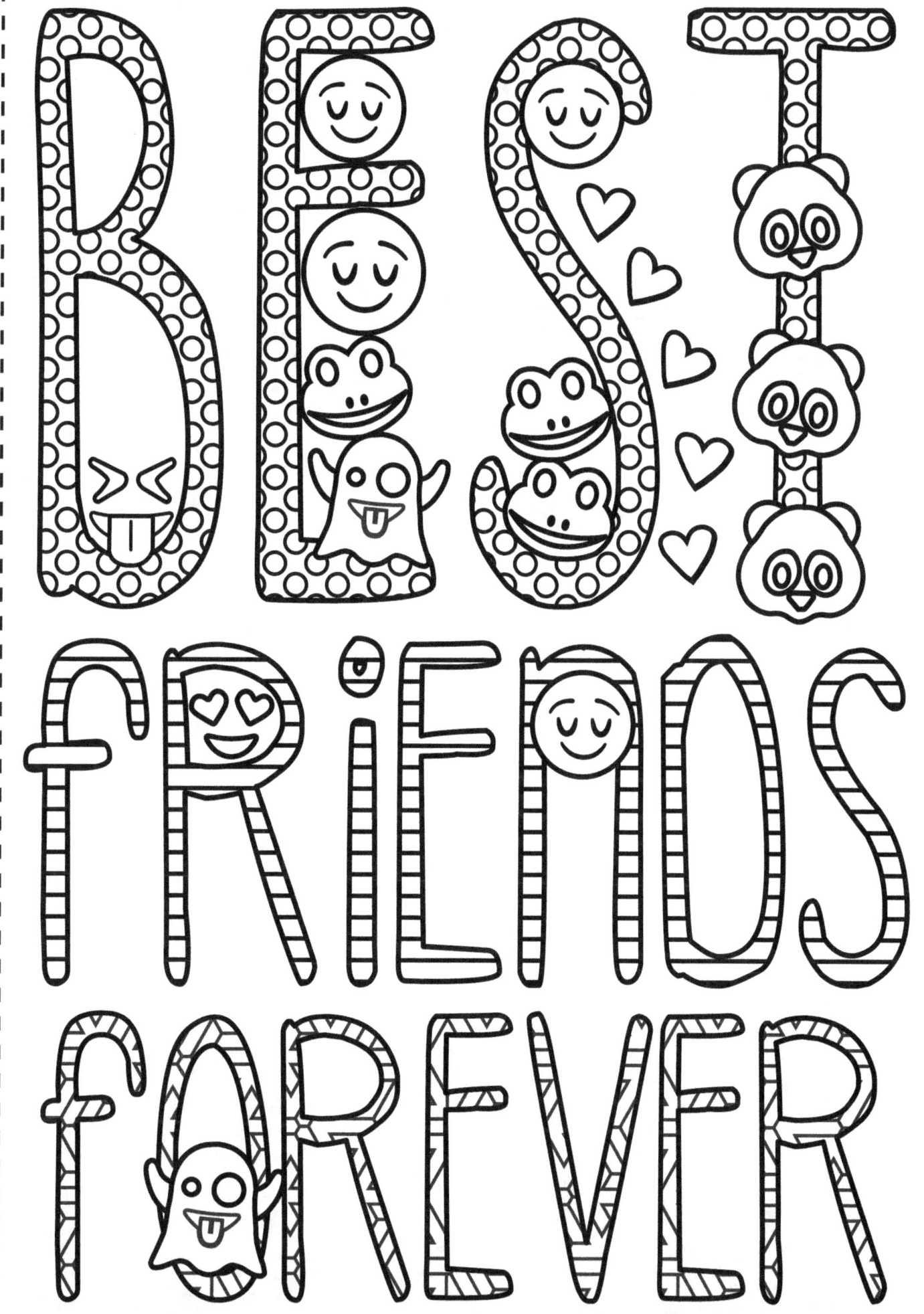

SPRINKLES

BEST FRIENDS

Best Friends

Best Friends

B F

SPRINKLES

BEST FRIENDS

F

Best Friends

FRIENDS FOREVER

Best Friends

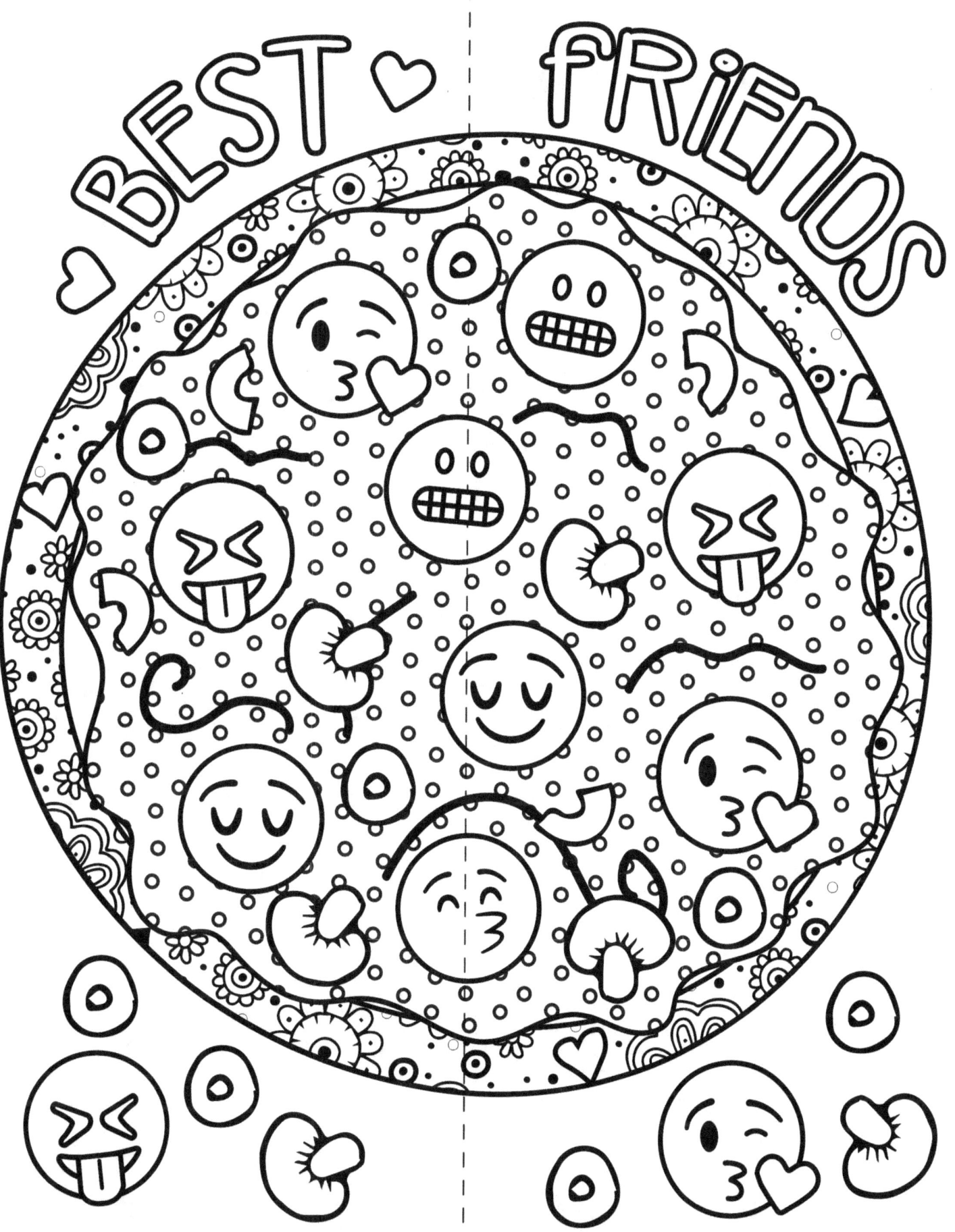

Cut along the dotted line. 1/2 for you, 1/2 for a friend
Or give your friend 1 copy and keep 1 for yourself. Color the whole pizza and then cut it in half, swap them and tape them back up!

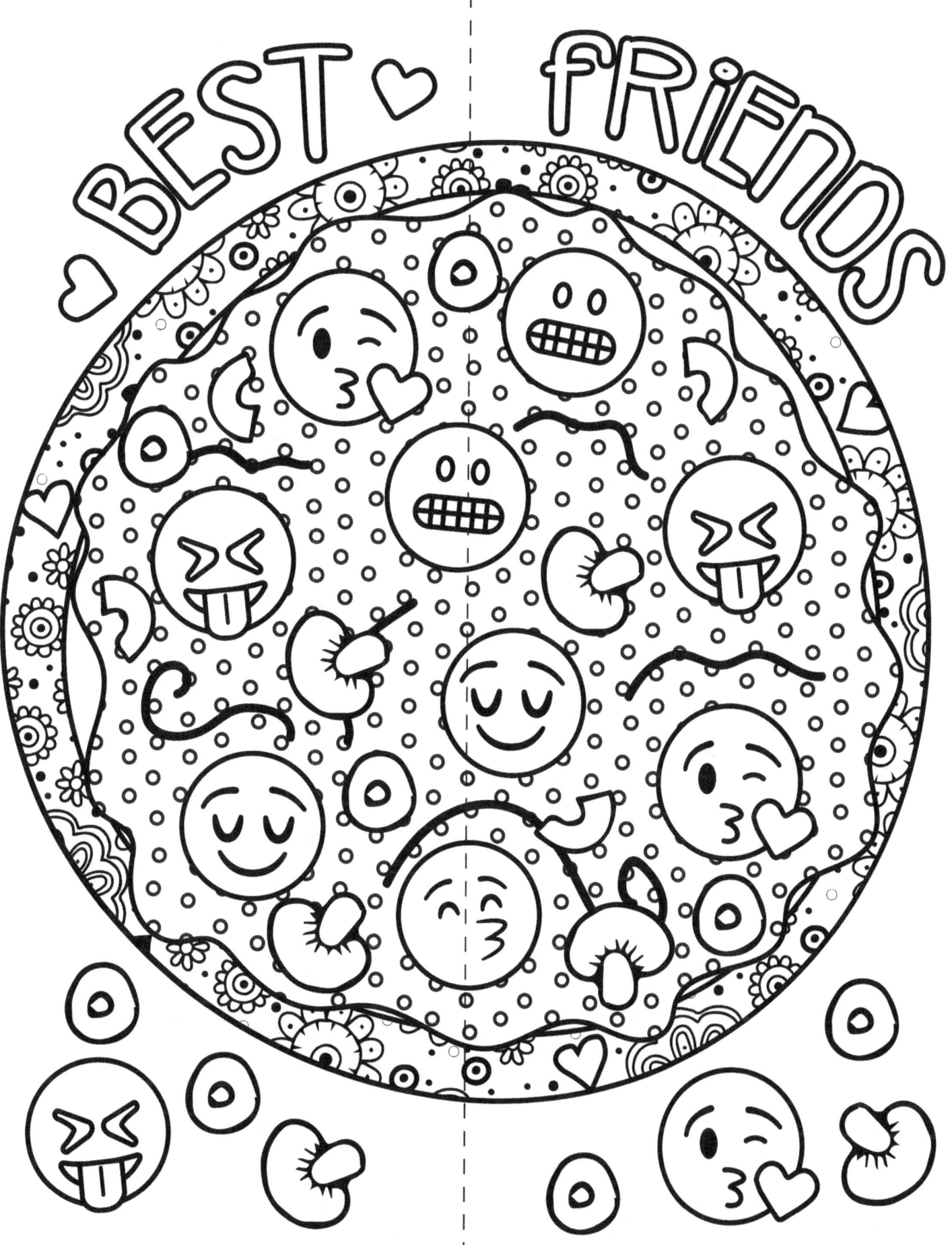

Cut along the dotted line. 1/2 for you, 1/2 for a friend
Or give your friend 1 copy and keep 1 for yourself. Color the whole pizza and then cut it in half, swap them and tape them back up!

YOU'RE THE PEANUT TO MY BUTTER THE *STAR* TO MY *BURST* THE POP* TO MY TART THE FRUIT TO MY LOOP AND THE BEST TO MY FRIEND!

YOU'RE THE PEANUT TO MY BUTTER THE *STAR* TO MY BURST THE POP TO MY TART THE FRUIT TO MY LOOP AND THE BEST TO MY FRIEND!

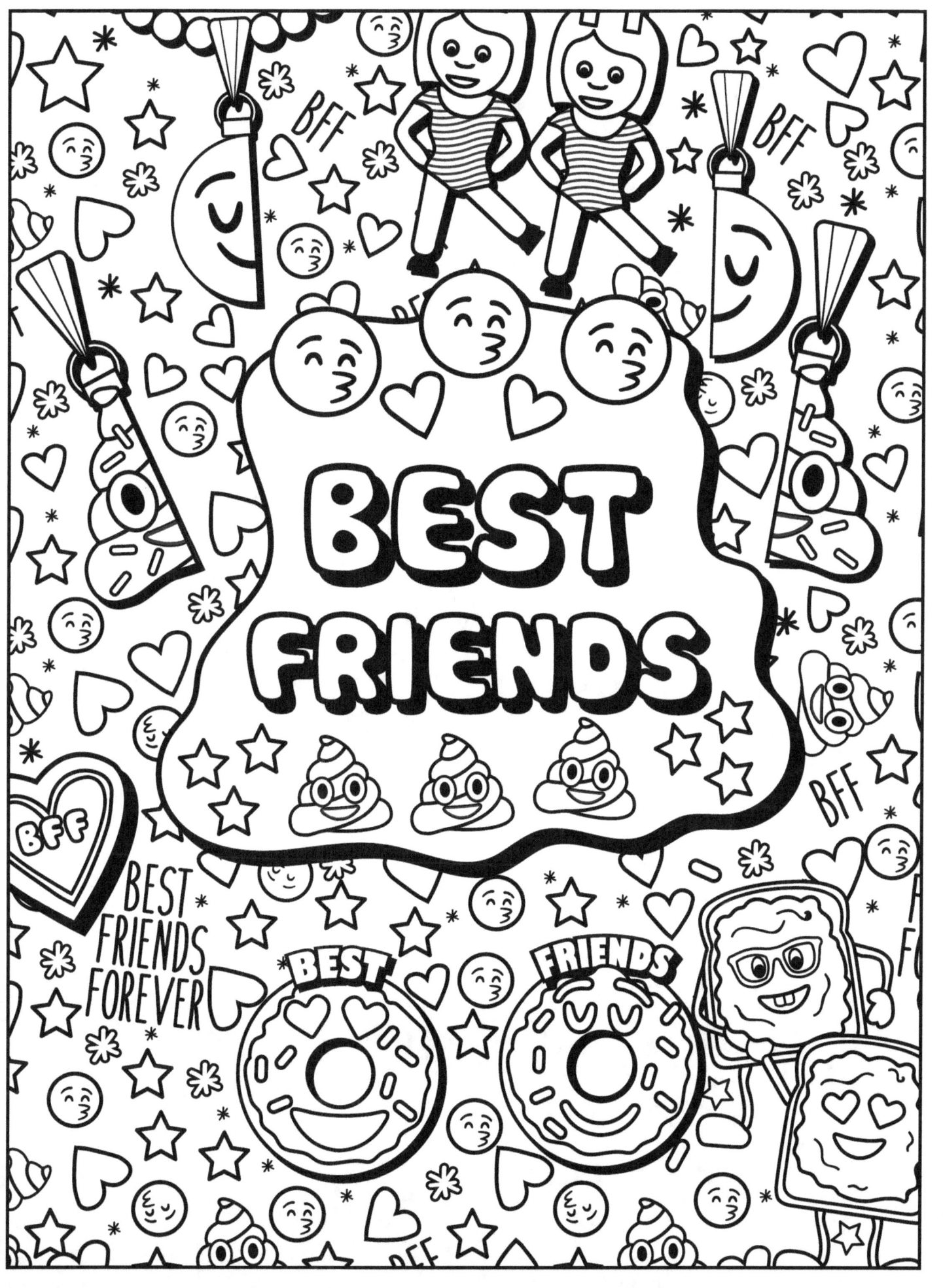

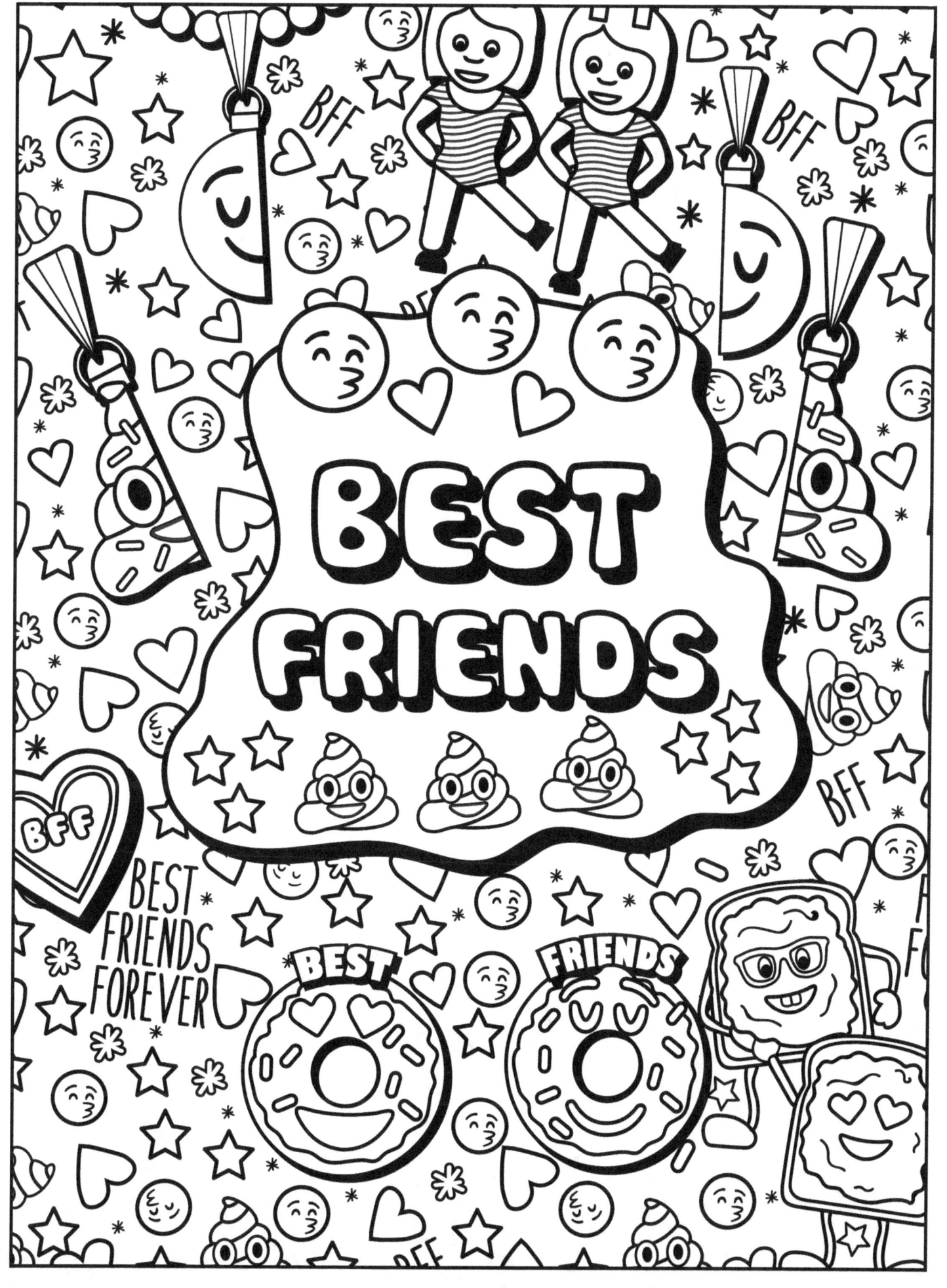

WE GO TOGETHER LIKE

MILK

MILK

MILK

and

WE GO TOGETHER LIKE

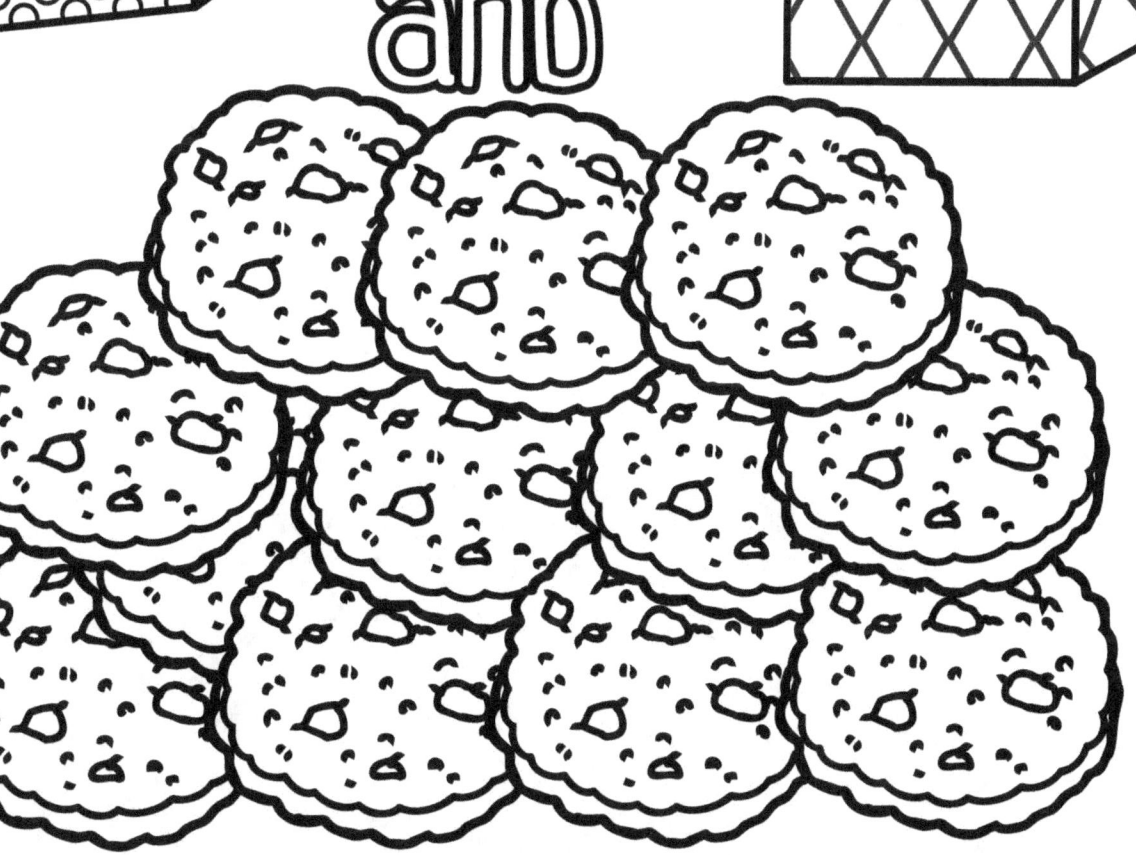

MILK MILK MILK

and

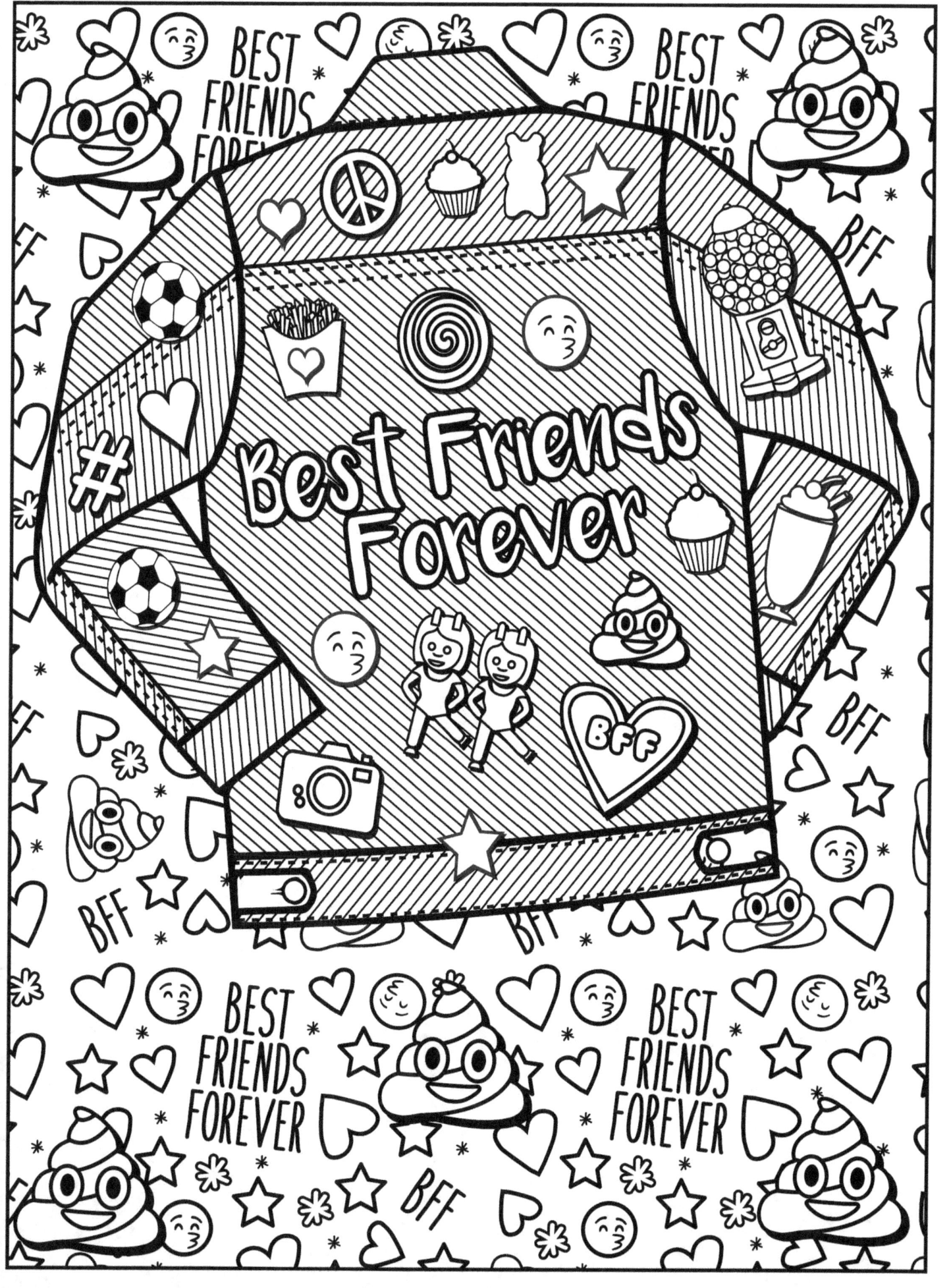

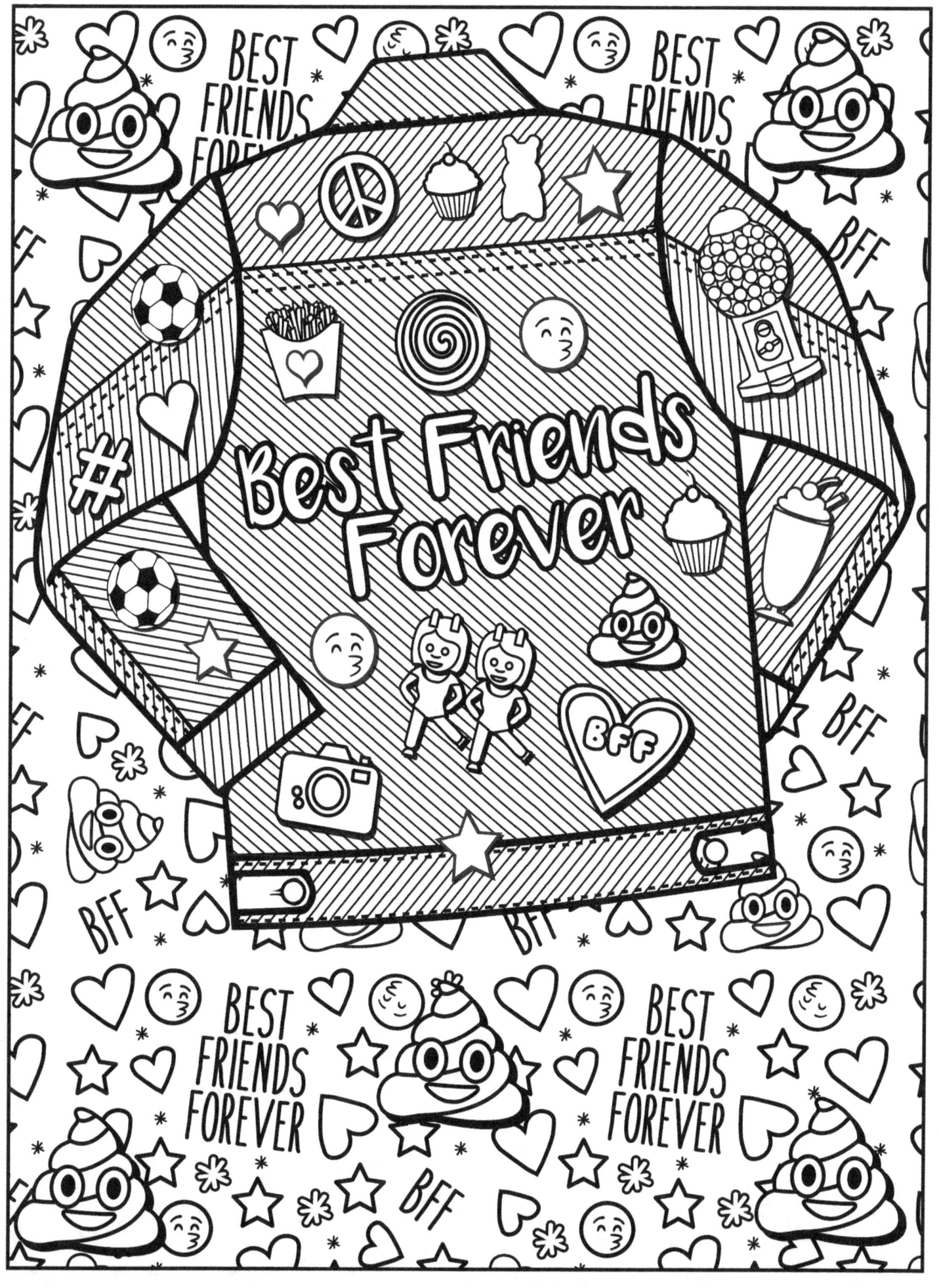

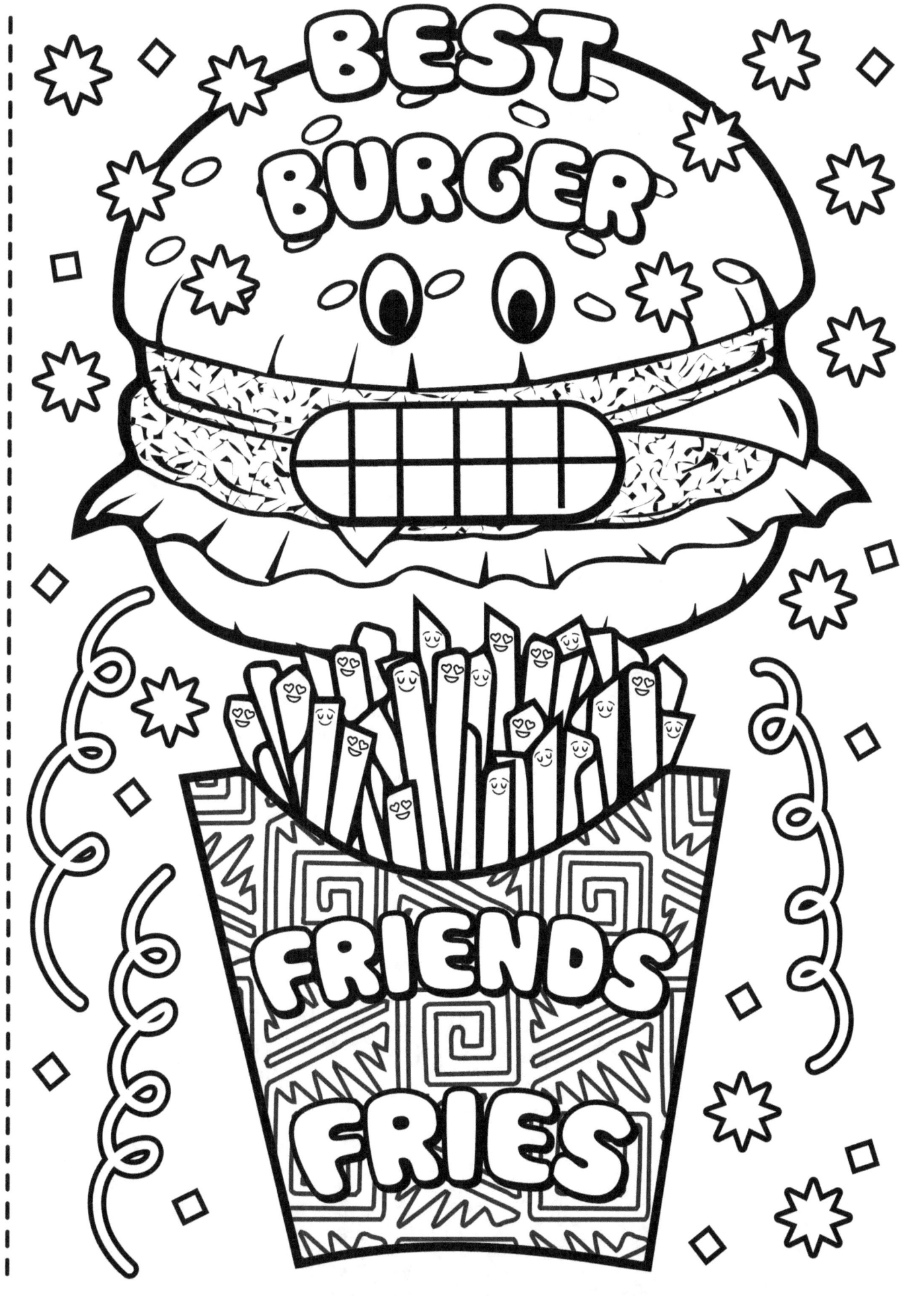

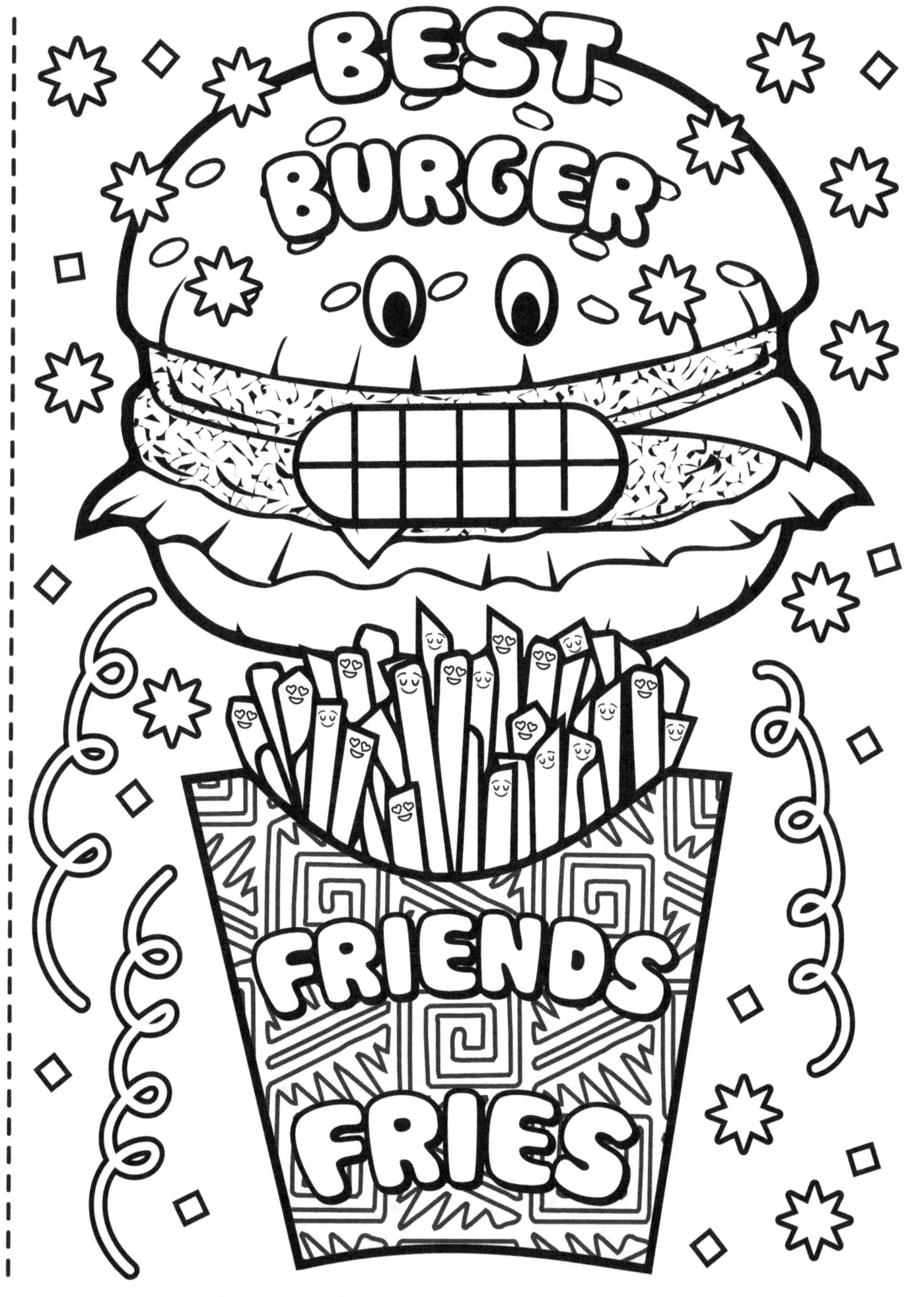

BEST FRIENDS

BFF

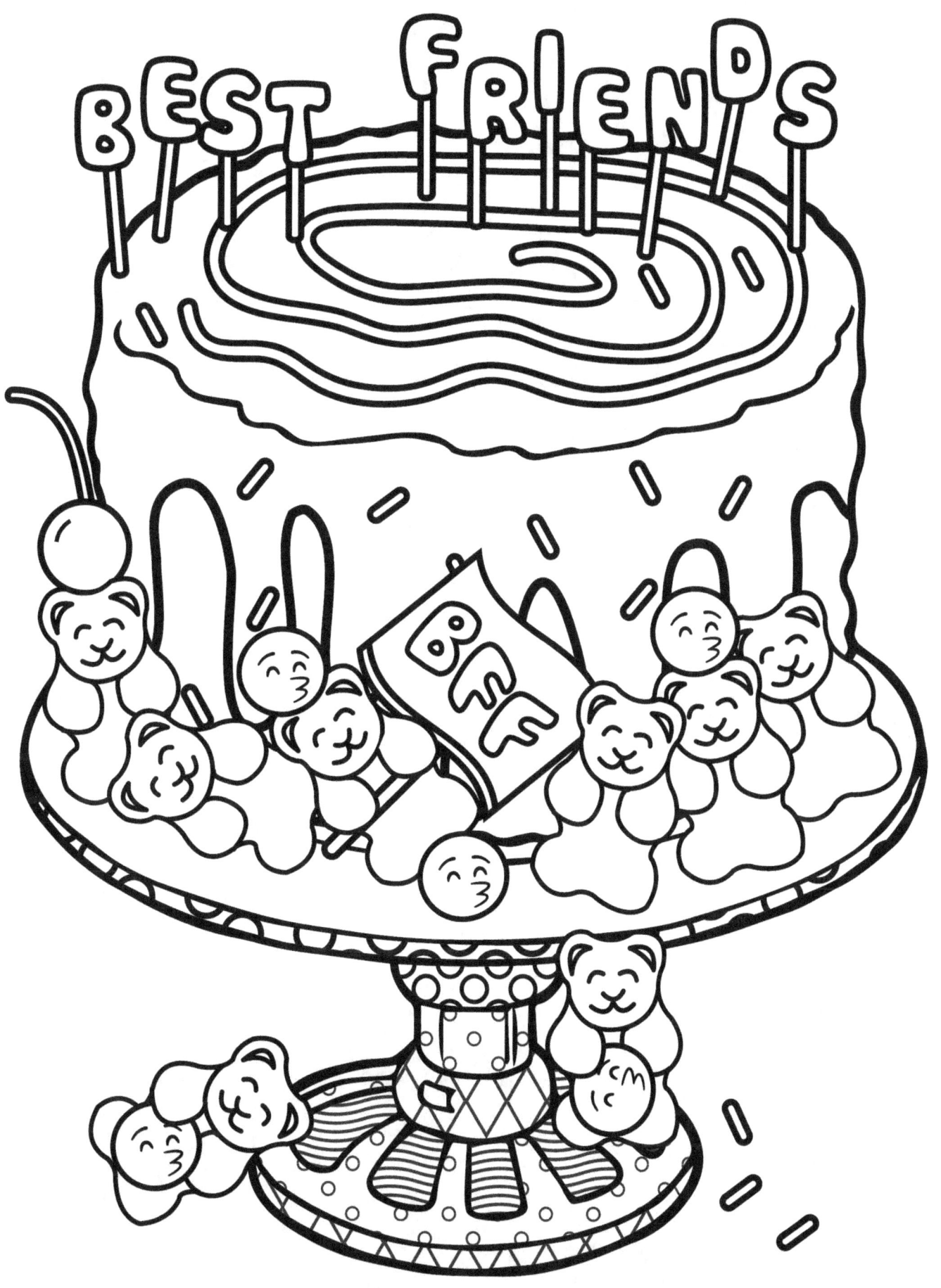

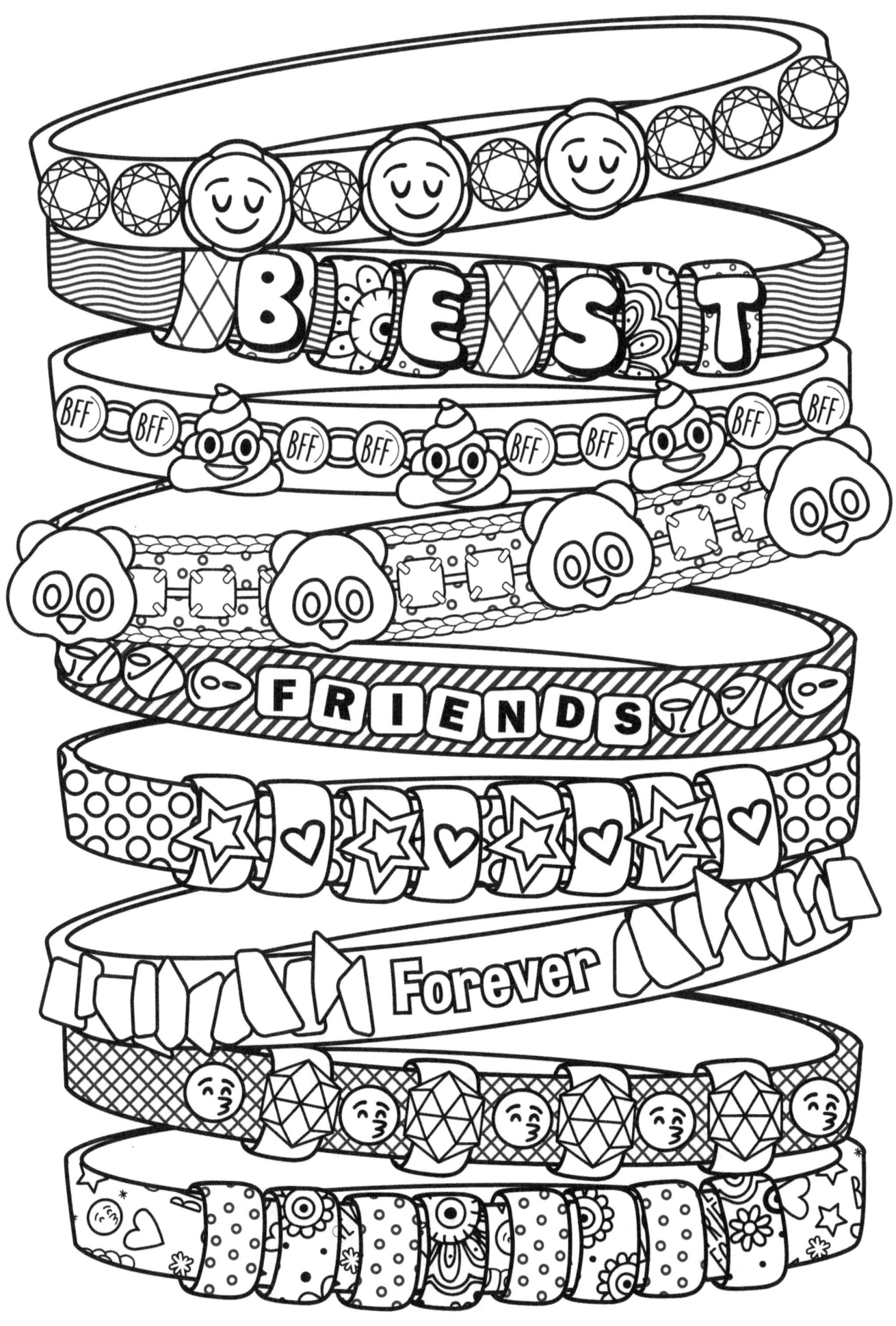

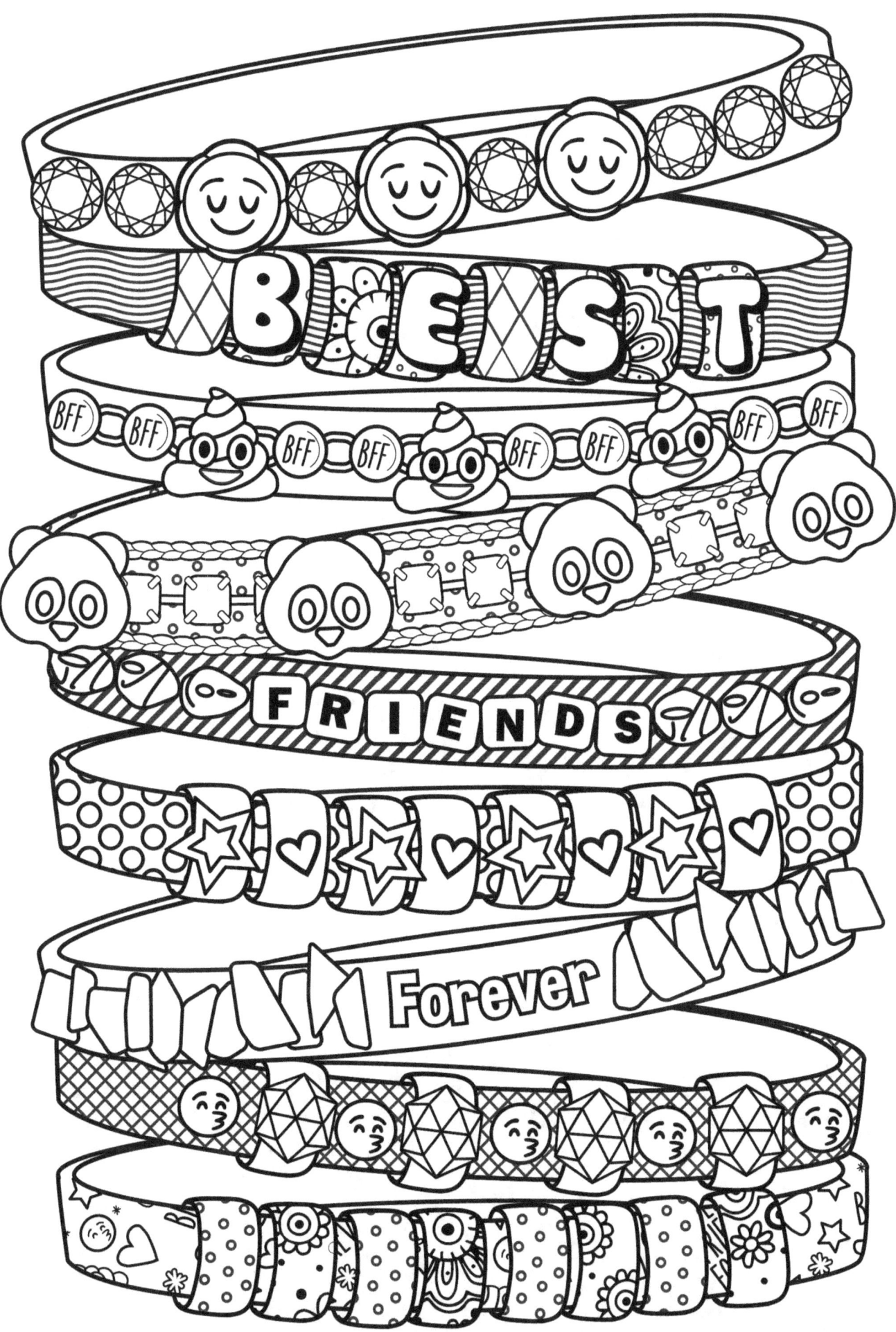

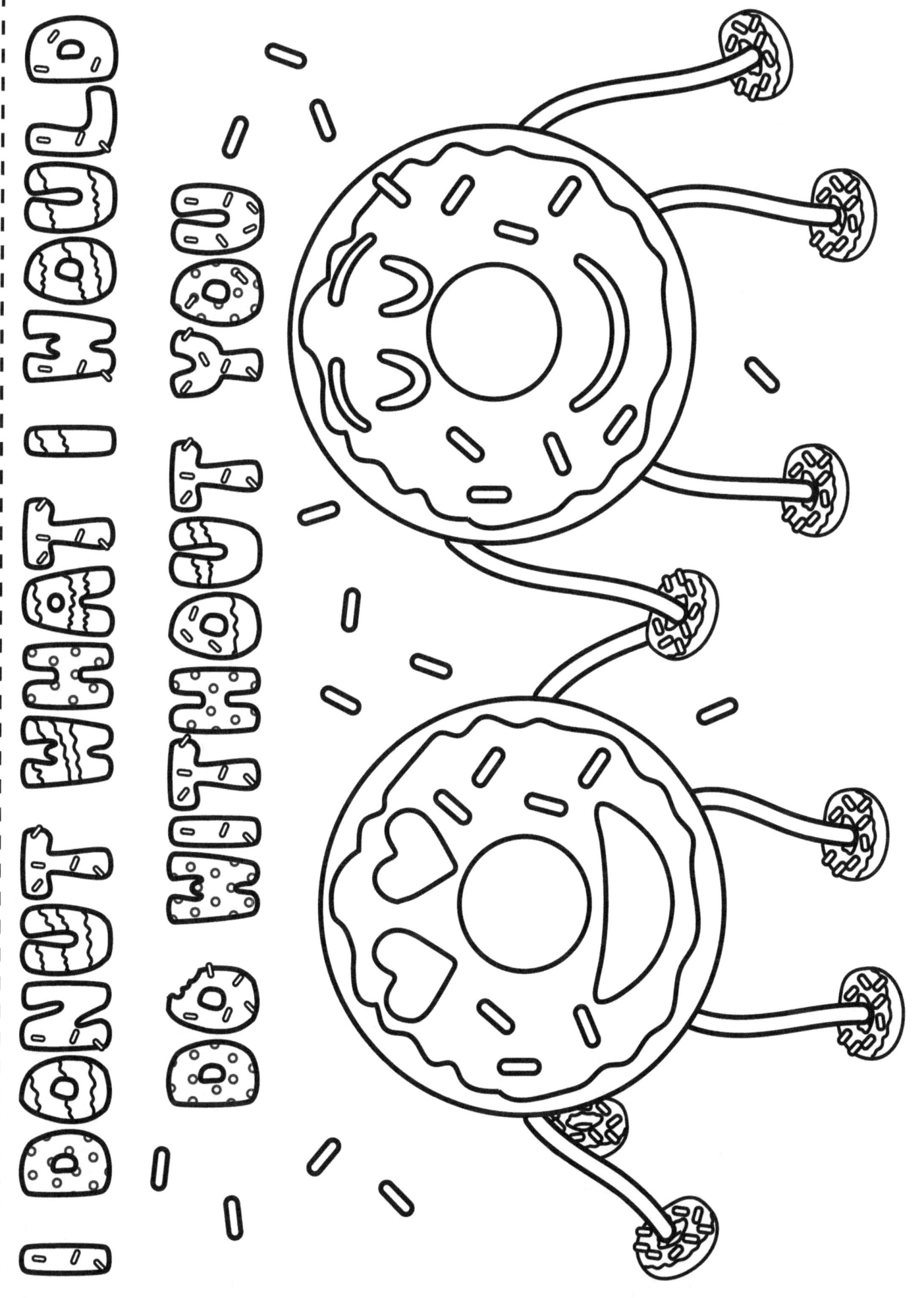

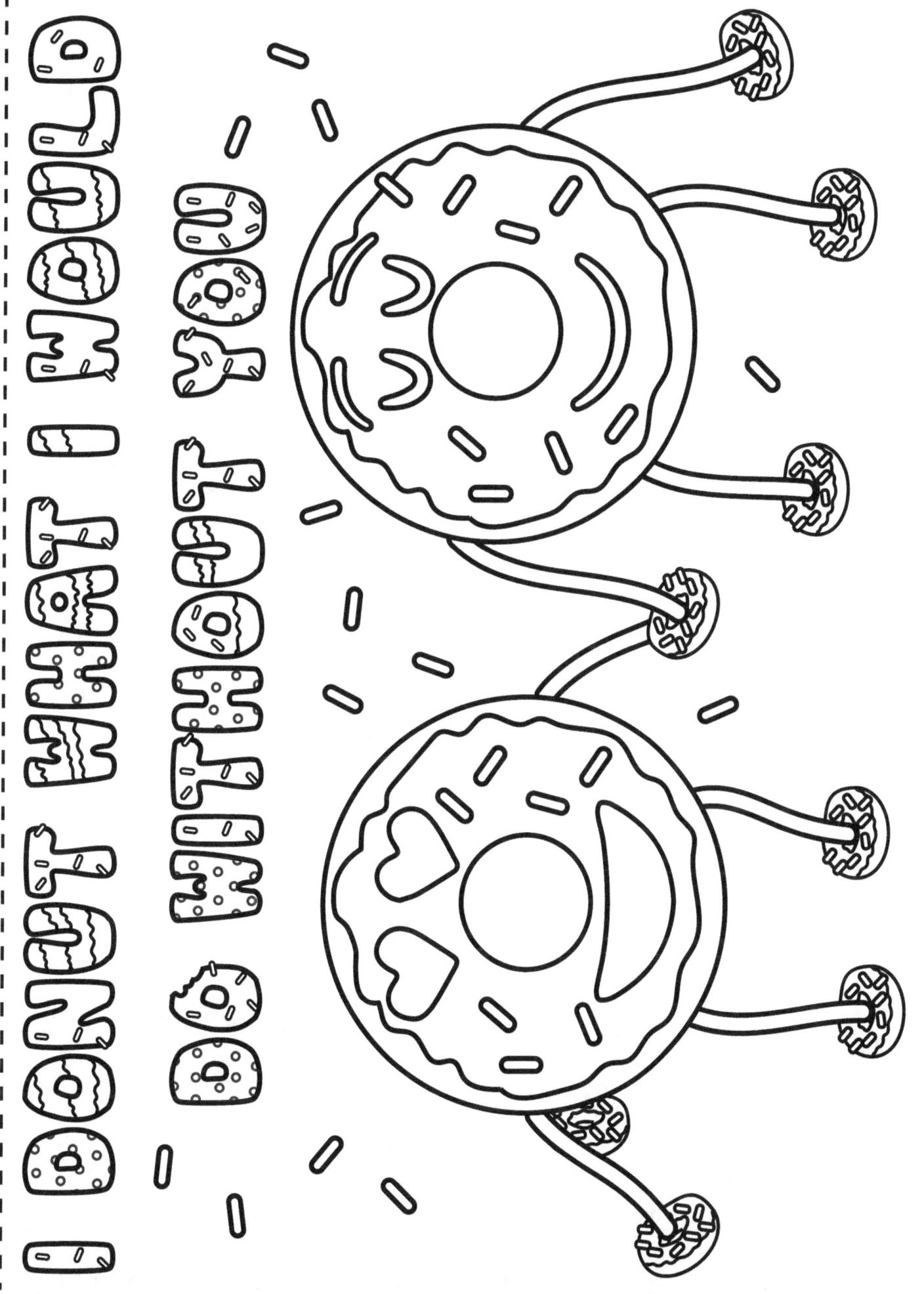

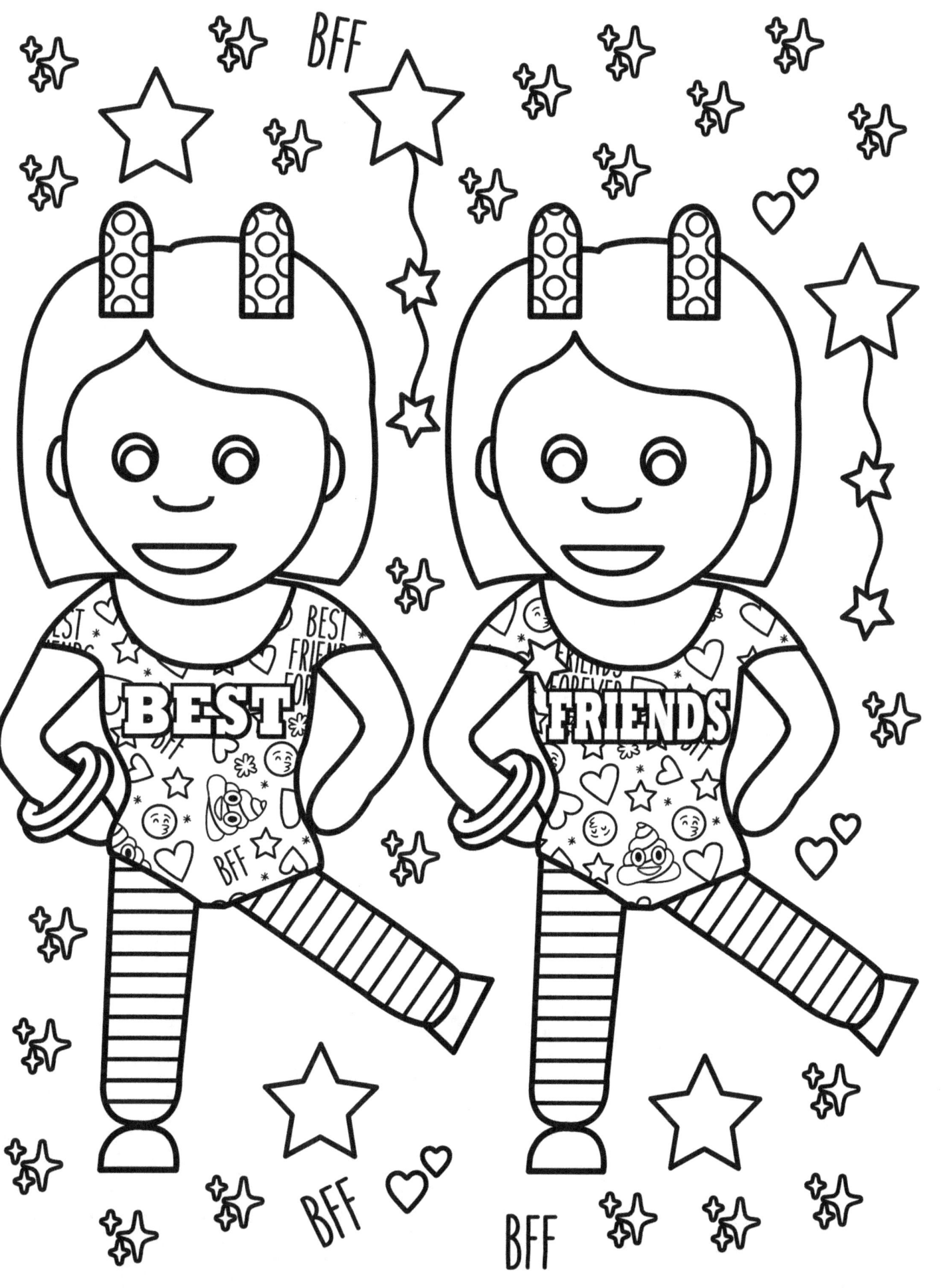

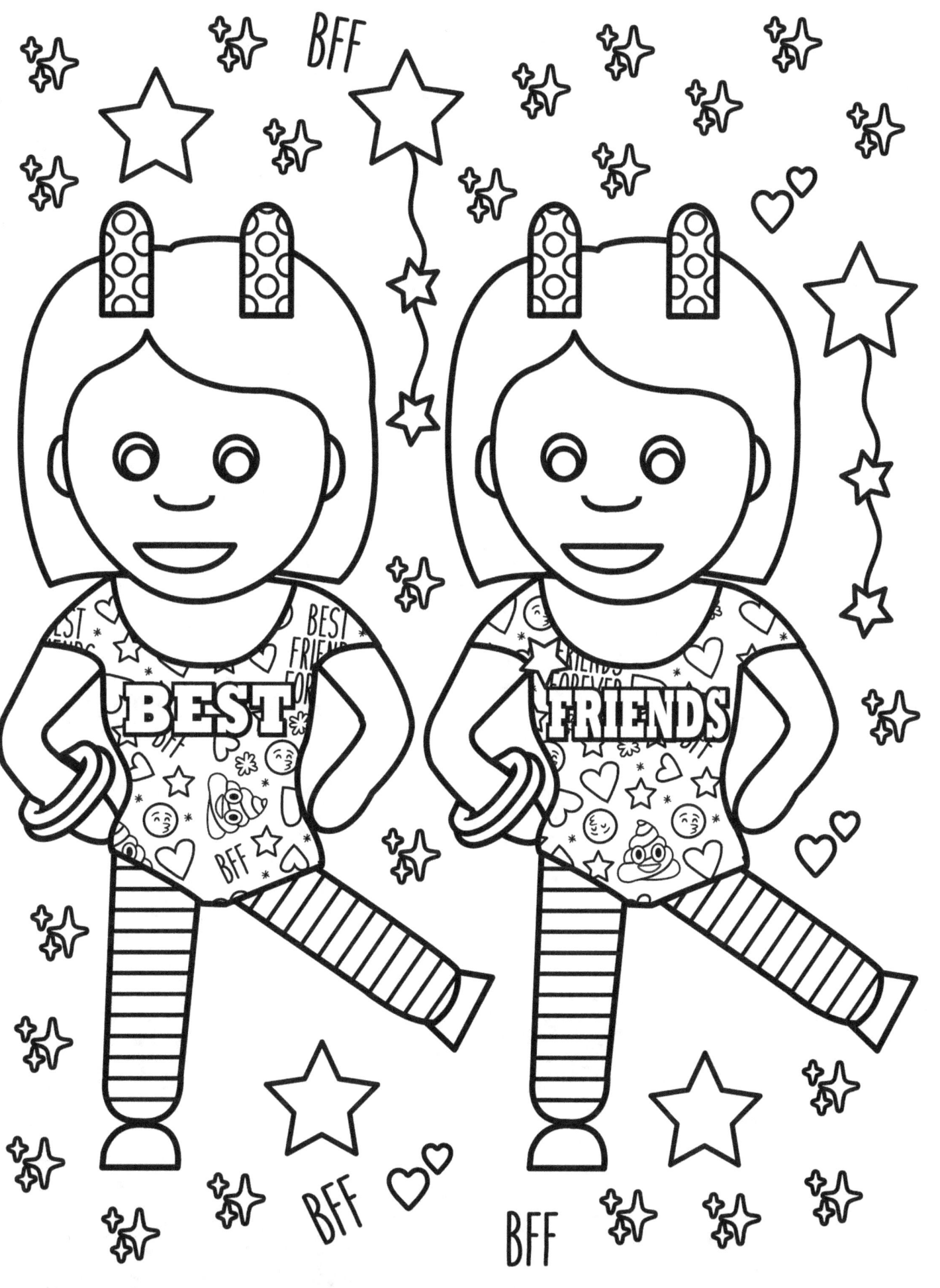

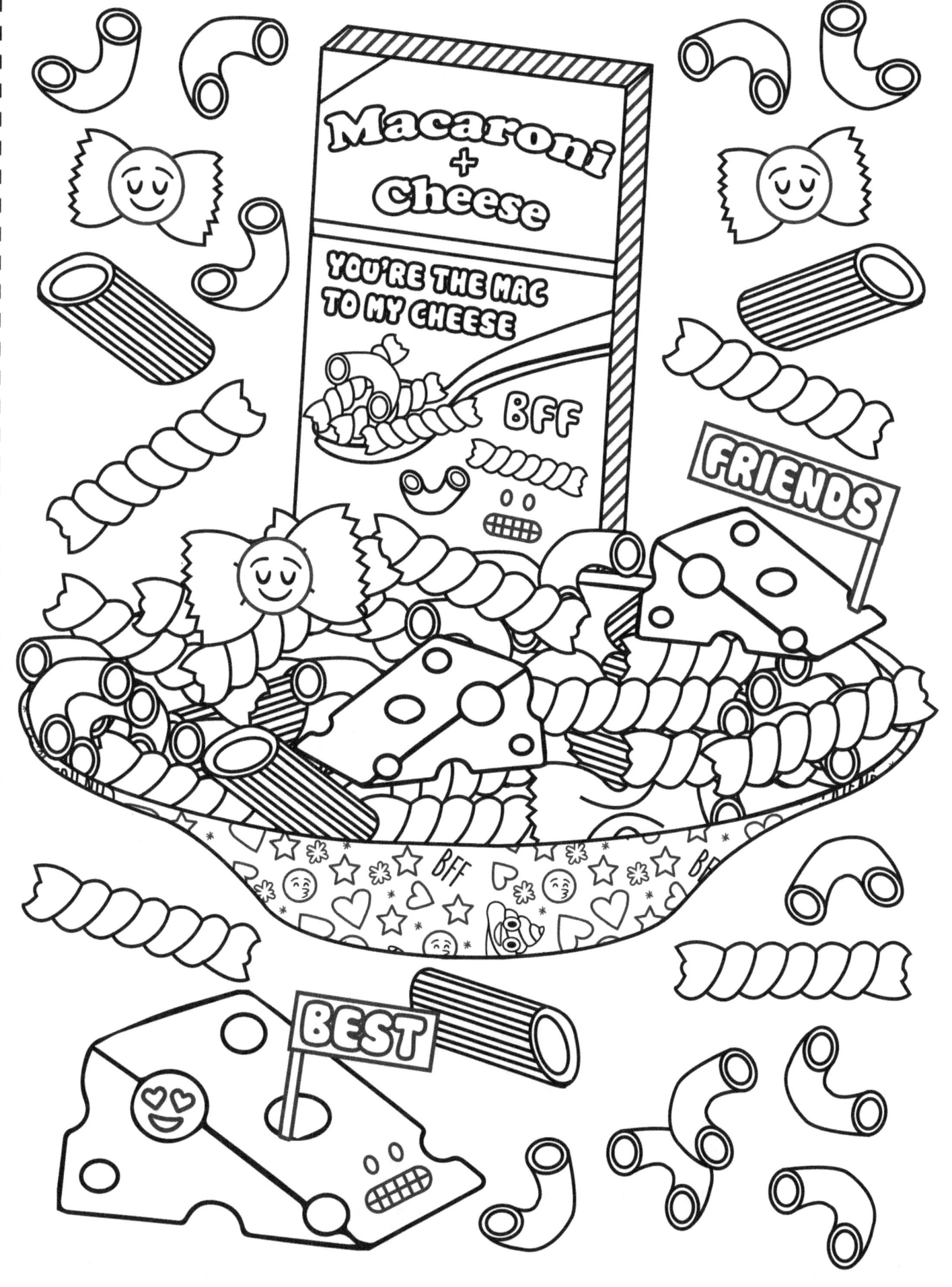

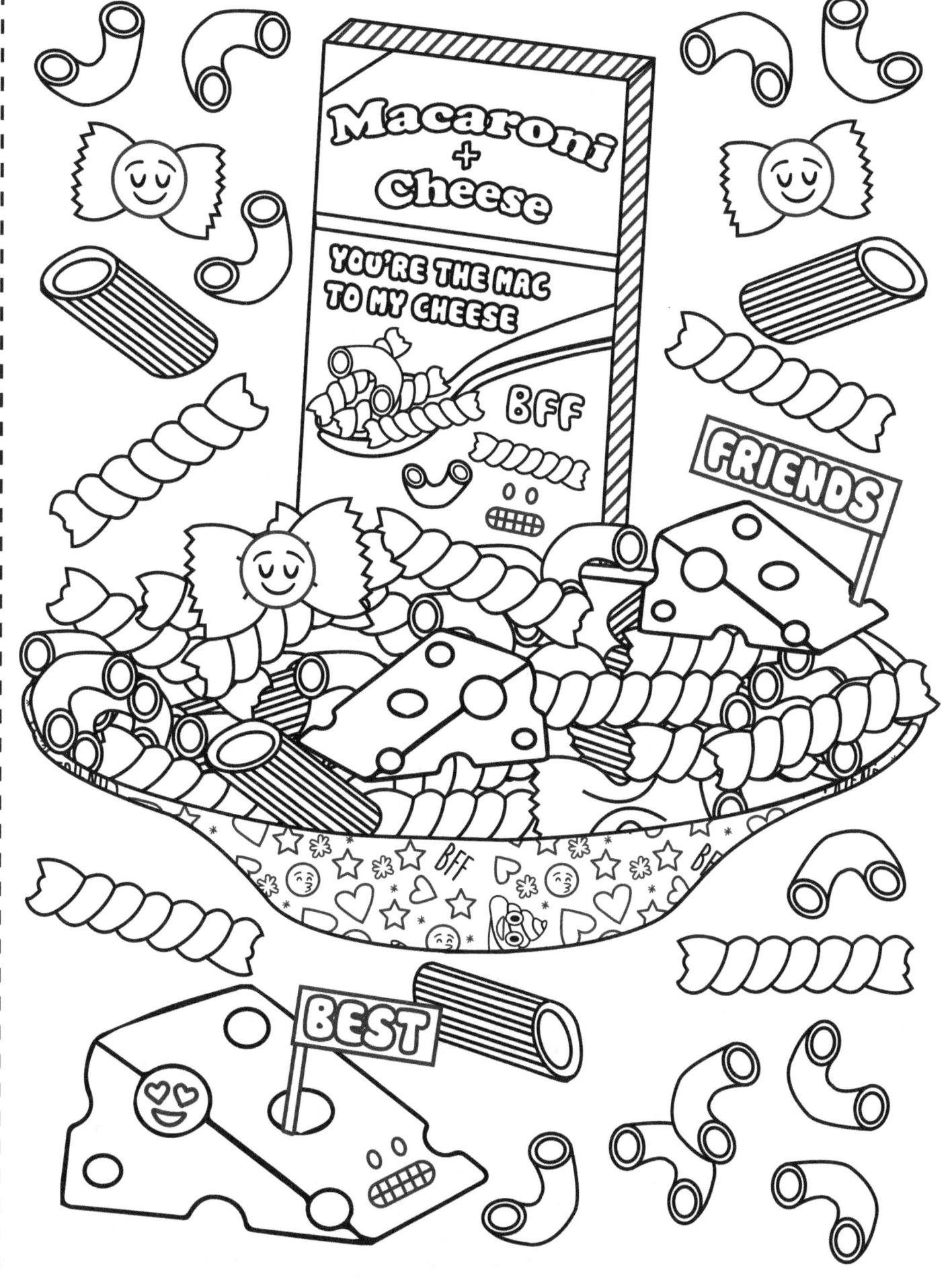

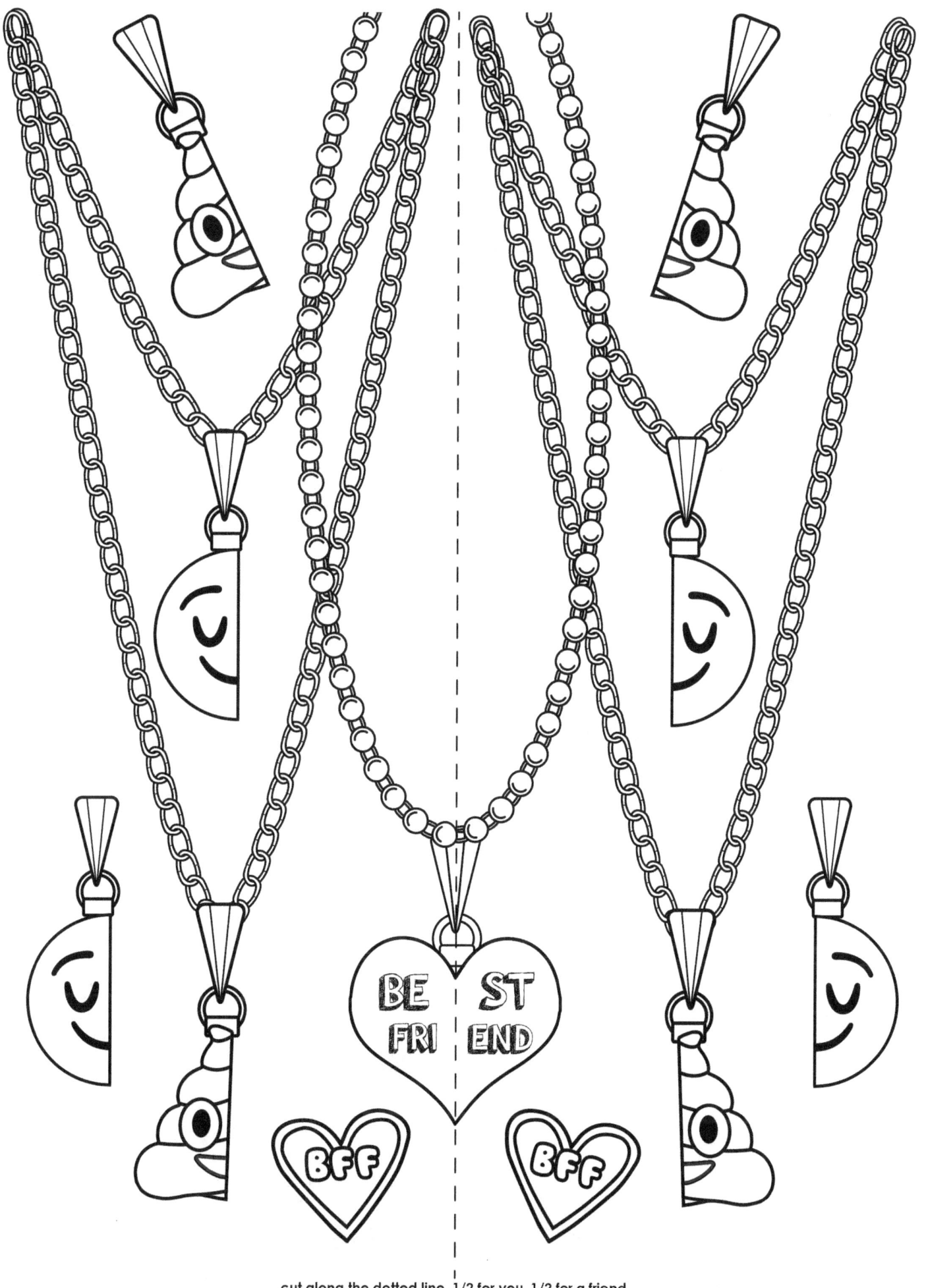

cut along the dotted line. 1/2 for you, 1/2 for a friend

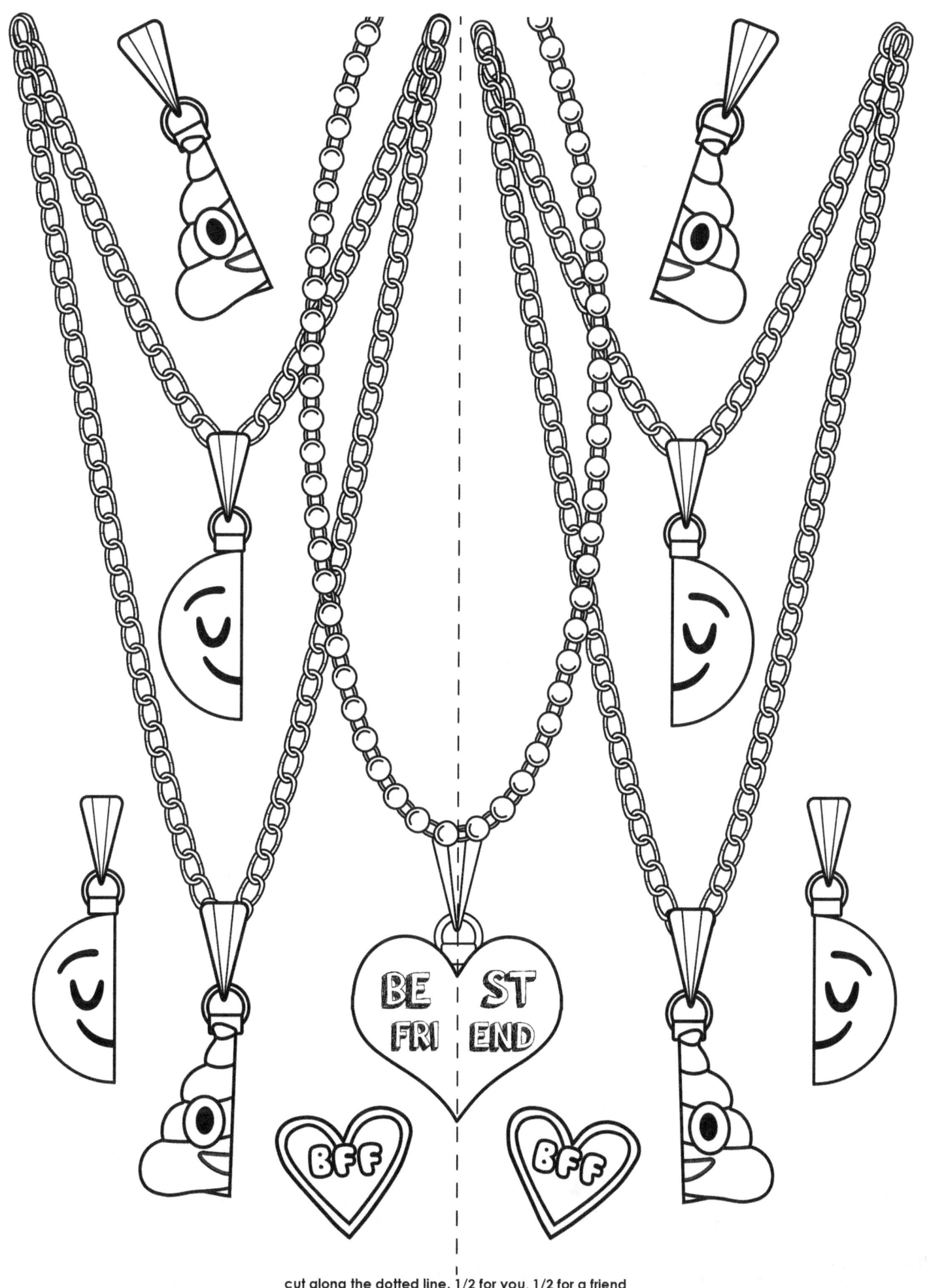

cut along the dotted line. 1/2 for you, 1/2 for a friend